SMALL GROUPS: Together We Can Grow

FORD MADISON
with STEVE WEBB

This book is designed for your personal reading pleasure and profit. It is also designed for group study. A leader's guide with helps and hints for teachers and visual aids (Victor Multiuse Transparency Masters) is available from your local bookstore or from the publisher.

VICTOR BOOKS

a division of SP Publications, Inc.

WHEATON. ILLINOIS 60187

Offices also in Fullerton, California • Whitby, Ontario, Canada • Amersham-on-the-Hill, Bucks, England

Recommended Dewey Decimal Classification: 248.4
    Suggested Subject Headings: Christian Life

Library of Congress Catalog Card Number: 80-51629
ISBN: 0-88207-223-4

VICTOR BOOKS
A division of SP Publications, Inc.
P.O. Box 1825 • Wheaton, Illinois 60187

Dedicated to the great men and women who,
through small fellowship groups,
have shared their lives—
including joys, hurts, and victories—
in seeking to follow Christ.

Most won't make the front page or the
5 o'clock news, but these ordinary
people have enriched my life
and many others through fellowship.

CONTENTS

FOREWORD

The author of this book first befriended me five years ago when we visited for a few hours of Bible study and fellowship. Since then my appreciation of, and affection for, Ford Madison has grown steadily.

In the pages of this thoughtful book, readers will come to know a man who has been a dear friend to many Christians, and who here sets forth some helpful suggestions for enhancing the fellowship of the saints.

Small Groups: Together We Can Grow should prove useful as a basic primer for beginning Christians eager to develop the discipline of personal and group fellowship. It is my hope that the volume will also help many to better understand the Christian faith, and to exhort many believers toward a deepened maturity in the body of Christ.

The support and direction provided by the small group of believers who surrounded me after my conversion to Christ was immeasurably important. Through them, I was grounded in the truths of Scripture; I was protected from doctrinal error and aided in spiritual growth; and I was introduced for the first time to those dimensions of love and fellowship which flow from hearts renewed in Jesus Christ.

All of us as Christians need the encouragement of fellow believers. Ford Madison's book should enrich the lives of many Christians seeking to glorify God together, and to be knit more closely in the household of faith.

Charles W. Colson

Be encouraged by the Apostle Paul who wrote:
Brothers, think of what you were when you were
called. Not many of you were wise by human
standards; not many were influential; not many
were of noble birth. But God chose the foolish
things of the world to shame the wise; God chose
the weak things of the world to shame the strong.
He chose the lowly things of this world and the
despised things—and the things that are not—to
nullify the things that are, so that no one may
boast before Him. It is because of Him that you
are in Christ Jesus, who has become for us wisdom
from God—that is, our righteousness, holiness,
and redemption. Therefore, as it is written:
"Let him who boasts boast in the Lord."

1 Corinthians 1:26-31, NIV

ONE

Fellowship— How Can I Get Some?

One evening my telephone rang. On the other end was a stranger's voice asking if we might have lunch together. "I've been reading about Christian fellowship," he explained, "and I'd like to know where I could get some."

After we met and got acquainted, I asked Richard Jones (not his real name) to tell me about his relationship with God. For years, he had been on the fringes of faith. As a young boy he had attended Sunday School. Subsequently, he became an adult Sunday School teacher and an elder in his church. But it was not till several years later, through reading books, that his faith was stirred.

While reading Catherine Marshall's *Something More* (Avon), Richard realized there was something missing in his life. In his business he was accustomed to bargaining. Utilizing the main tool he knew, Richard tried to make a deal with God. He would turn over his life to God on his 44th birthday.

As the date approached, he didn't discuss it with anyone. Finally the big day arrived. After a family birthday dinner he started up the stairs to his bedroom. With heavy feet he trudged up the steps, closed the door, and knelt by the bed. There he followed Catherine Marshall's suggestion and through prayer committed as much of his life as he understood to as much of God as he knew.

Richard became a new person inside. The spirit of Christ entered his heart and life. Richard's reading continued with new meaning. His Bible and books about Christian life took on added significance. Many of these books alluded to the idea of fellowship with other believers.

During our lunch, Richard expressed his frustration with the concept of fellowship. He sensed from the books he was reading that the authors were experiencing something that was escaping him. Fellowship was something he hadn't consistently experienced in any of the organizations he had been in, nor even in his social club, where the same couples had met monthly for 20 years.

Richard related how he had also called his pastor and asked to meet with him for "fellowship." They agreed to meet together on Monday mornings. After a few weeks, the pastor cancelled the meetings.

Richard still hadn't found the fellowship he had read about. He still ached for it. How could he get some? I laughed because I thought there was a simple answer, and in one sense there is. Yet, as it did Richard, that answer eludes many of us and causes unnecessary frustration.

In the years that have passed since that luncheon conversation, I have found the concept of fellowship to be a very profound subject. The Lord has called all believers into fellowship with His Son, Jesus Christ (1 Cor. 1:9). Fellowship, then, is the sum and substance of the Christian life. It describes our most basic relationship with God, and hopefully, with one another. This should include sharing, giving, serving, and caring. But let's start by looking at the basics which can make these a greater reality.

How Fellowship Begins

Biblical fellowship starts as a three-way proposition. All that is required is you, others, and God. The Apostle John described it in 1 John 1:3, "What we have seen and heard we proclaim to you also, that you also may have fellowship with us; and indeed our fellowship is with the Father, and with His Son Jesus Christ." John told believers that in order to experience fellowship with each other, they first had to have fellowship with Christ.

John was expounding a principle already set forth by Jesus. The Lord said, "Where two or three have gathered together in My name, there I am in their midst" (Matt. 18:20). This statement is an expression of Christ's desire to have fellowship with groups of believers. That He is speaking only of believers is clear through His words, "gathered *in My name.*"

But why are two or three people necessary? Because certain dimensions of spiritual growth require other people. We cannot do it all alone and come to maturity. We are all part of a spiritual posse. We can't survive as the Lone Ranger. We need God and other believers to experience fellowship.

The Lord takes special notice when a group of people come together in His name. Fellowship is so important to God that Malachi indicates that God actually keeps a divine record of such meetings. "Then those who feared the Lord spoke to one another, and the Lord gave attention and heard it, and a book of remembrance was written before Him for those who fear the Lord and who esteem His name. 'And they will be Mine' says the Lord of hosts, 'on the day that I prepare My own possession, and I will spare them as a man spares his own son who serves him' " (Mal. 3:16-17).

To experience fellowship a person must be a believer in Christ first, then meet with other believers in the name of Christ. This is the beginning of fellowship. But before we explore further aspects of it, let us lay to rest any preconceived ideas we may have about fellowship. Let's see how fellowship is not initiated.

How Fellowship Doesn't Begin

Fellowship is not just sitting down to coffee and donuts, nor even a dinner. It *can* happen in that kind of setting, though, and is often facilitated by sharing a meal together. But just eating a meal together doesn't produce fellowship any more than would riding on an elevator together.

Picture people grouped together in an elevator all headed for the same floor. There is no interaction, no communication. Staring at the elevator door does not produce fellowship. So also in businesses, clubs, and sometimes even in church organizations—there's a missing element.

Too often fellowship is portrayed as getting together with someone else. This is only *one* of the requirements. A more important prerequisite exists. We must first be together with God through the Lord Jesus Christ. Once we establish and maintain this relationship vertically, then true fellowship results on a horizontal plane.

Christ opens the spiritual dimension on the horizontal level. The result of His light is fellowship with all others who share His light. He is the basic dynamic in fellowship. If He is missing, fellowship just doesn't happen!

"But if we walk in the light as He Himself is in the light, we have fellowship with one another, and the blood of Jesus His Son cleanses us from all sin" (1 John 1:7). Fellowship is a triangular relationship which exists when at least two believers meet together who already are walking with God.

What Fellowship Requires

First, we must establish our relationship with God. When Richard Jones knelt by his bedside on his 44th birthday, he established that relationship and began to experience God's fellowship. Christ says there is only one way to come to God, that He Himself is the Way (John 14:6). Christ came primarily to be our Sacrifice. Jesus said that He would be lifted up so that we might have eternal life (John 3:14-15). He was lifted up on a wooden cross, and although He personally had not done anything wrong, He was executed. God designed this to be the payment for all the sins of mankind (1 Peter 2:24). Jesus sacrificed His life for us, that we might live.

When any person believes the Word of God that the death of Christ is God's provision for his sin, then a supernatural transaction happens. That person's sins are forgiven and his relationship with God is established. This was the transaction Richard Jones experienced. He realized his sins were forgiven, and the first prerequisite had been met.

Remember John's words, "What we have seen and heard we proclaim to you also, that you also may have fellowship with us; and indeed our fellowship is with the Father, and with His Son Jesus Christ" (1 John 1:3). The incomprehensible fact is that God wants fellowship with us!

In His great love, God desires an intimate relationship with us. He does not want to wait till we get to heaven to have our fellowship. He wants it now. That is why He provided His Son to pay the penalty for our sin, so we could have the foundation for fellowship with *Him!*

Before we discover how fellowship works, let's examine the most important of all relationships. Do we have the spirit of Christ living in us? (Rom. 8:9) The Lord Jesus Christ will come into our lives if we invite Him. We can be sure by opening the door to our hearts and through prayer, asking Jesus Christ to enter. He has promised, "Behold, I stand at the door and knock; if any one hears My voice and opens the door, I will come in to him, and will dine with him, and he with Me" (Rev. 3:20).

In Christ's words, we see the foundation for all true fellowship—a relationship with God through Christ. When this relationship has been established, we are brought together with other believers from every race and nation (Rev. 5:9). Being a member of the family of God transcends any human barrier that separates us.

The second essential for fellowship is to walk in God's light. Let us consider the one spiritual cause for separation. Sin separates. I can still have my salvation but be out of fellowship with God. I am either carnal (walking in the flesh), or spiritual (walking in the light).

The directive will of God is like a bright spotlight moving across the darkened stage of life. My job is to stay in that spotlight. If I stand still, the spotlight may go off and leave me. If I move too fast I'll get ahead of it. If I veer to the left or right, I'll miss it. Paul said since we live by the Spirit, let's keep in step with the Spirit (Gal. 5:25). Part of the great Good News is that we not only have forgiveness and cleansing from heaven, but that we can experience it today as we move across our stage of life. The result of this love-cleansed relationship with God is fellowship with other believers.

How to Maintain Fellowship

Christ said that if we continue in the Word, then we are God's disciples indeed (John 8:31). Continuing involves learning God's words and receiving them as the Holy Spirit interprets them and applies them to our own lives.

All Scripture is given by inspiration of God and is profitable for many things (2 Tim. 3:16). The same Holy Spirit that moved men to speak and record the inerrant Word of God can also move *us* to understand the spiritual meaning of the Bible. This is why it is important to approach the Scriptures with a prayerful, believing attitude. "Open Thou mine eyes, that I may behold wondrous things out of Thy law" (Ps. 119:18, KJV).

The perspective of the person who believes the Scriptures is very different from one who doesn't. The story of the man who was given any wish he wanted well illustrates this. When the man made his wish, he drew on his business savvy for a wise choice. He chose to have a look at the stock market page one year from that day. That would give him all the answers for life.

His wish was granted. Zealously, the man took notes on the stock prices. As he scanned the last column, the adjoining section of the newspaper caught his eye. There were the obituaries. And there, to his dismay, was his own picture and the story of his own death.

The perspective of the one seeking riches is much different from that of someone who recognizes biblical values and seeks God's will. It is not earthly wisdom we need but godly wisdom —that which is contained only in His Word. "The counsel of the Lord stands forever, the plans of His heart from generation to generation" (Ps. 33:11).

Studying the Word of God is the primary way that we can learn more about God. "For you have been born again not of seed which is perishable but imperishable, that is, through the living and abiding Word of God. For 'All flesh is like grass, and all its glory like the flower of grass. The grass withers, and the flower falls off but the Word of the Lord abides forever.' And this is the word which was preached to you" (1 Peter 1:23-25).

God has given us His very great and precious promises that "By them you might become partakers of the divine nature" (2 Peter 1:4). It is through God's promises that we can actually draw upon His nature. As we allow His thoughts to transform our minds, His Word again becomes flesh. In this way, believers can be models of an alternative lifestyle.

View the contrast in our world today between a young man and woman living with each other on a trial basis compared to a young man and woman committed to each other in Christian marriage. The superior lifestyle demonstrates a value system that makes loving God the number one priority. Seeking God's will first is the ultimate security system. Then to demonstrate His love wherever and with whomever He places us is the unselfish approach to life.

Hopefully, as we grow in Christ we will be recognized as being full of grace and truth. God's Word has always been able to transform lives. Jesus said that man should "not live on bread alone, but on every word that proceeds out of the mouth of God" (Matt. 4:4). Moses, in his final sermon, said, "Take to your heart all the words with which I am warning you today, which you shall command your sons to observe carefully, even all the words of this law. For it is not an idle word for you; indeed it is your life. And by this word you shall prolong your days in the land, where you are about to cross over the Jordan to possess it" (Deut. 32:46-47).

Satisfying Fellowship

If the fellowship group in which you are involved seems shallow and the conversation only concerns superficial matters, then it is likely that the Word of God is not central. As we filter our lives through the sieve of God's Word, God changes our outlook. We focus on the deeper meanings behind the events, circumstances, and relationships that touch our lives.

One friend has characterized fellowship groups in two categories. One group may be like a river a mile wide and an inch deep while the other group is like a river an inch wide and a mile deep. If the problem is the former, the way to dredge out the canal and get the waters of life flowing again is to liberally introduce the Word of God.

Exchanging thoughts with one another as an outgrowth of our individual study gives greater depth to fellowship. To achieve depth, a group's sharing and interaction must be biblically oriented. Discussing attitudes, decisions, and actions in light of God's Word will keep us from stumbling and muddling through life.

It is spiritually essential for each participant in a small fellowship group to be involved in learning God's Word. "Jesus therefore was saying to those Jews who had believed Him, 'If you abide in My word, then you are truly disciples of Mine'" (John 8:31). How else can one continue? If the fellowship is to function, then the light of Christ as revealed through the Bible must shine—for each participant. If Bible study is not part of a group's format, then the individual members need to be getting it somewhere else—in their individual study, as well as at their local churches or other Bible study groups.

The conversations with Richard Jones indicated he had established his relationship with God. But he hadn't discovered fellowship. He was seeking it primarily through books. The Book he needed was the Bible, God's inspired Word. He also needed other people looking to the same Source as their authority and for daily guidance through life. As the psalmist said, "Thy Word is a lamp to my feet, and a light to my path" (Ps. 119:105). The application of the Word of God to our lives is the way we turn on this light.

There are five ways for scriptural intake: hearing, reading, studying, memorizing, and meditating. When we attend church and Sunday School, we have the opportunity to *hear* God's Word. If we would set aside an average of 20 minutes a day we can *read* the whole Bible in a year. To understand more of God and to know Him better, we can *study* the Scriptures individually and with other people. The psalmist asked the question, "How can a young man keep his way pure?" and answered this question by suggesting a Scripture *memory* course. "Thy Word I have treasured in my heart, that I may not sin against Thee" (vv. 9, 11).

God told Joshua, "This book of the law shall not depart from your mouth, but you shall *meditate* (italics added) on it day and night, so that you may be careful to do according to all that is written in it; for then you will make your way prosperous, and then you will have success" (Josh. 1:8). Meditation is careful thought toward personal application—and the bottom line of the other four methods of intake. It's best if all five of these are utilized together. As Jesus said, "If you abide in My Word, then you are truly disciples of Mine; and you shall know the truth, and the truth shall make you free" (John 8:31-32).

These actions, however, mean nothing if we do not apply God's Word. All of our mental sweat will not produce fruit. But where we are willing to proclaim God's Word by physical, verbal, or spiritual application in our own lives, there will God produce.

TWO

Rejection Is Not an Option

Being born into a family does not give a baby an option to select his parents, brothers, or sisters. So also when we're born into God's spiritual family by receiving Christ we don't have the luxury of selecting our brothers and sisters. Anyone with the Spirit of Christ living within is part of God's family.

But how do we respond to our spiritual brothers and sisters? Do we accept others, encouraging spiritual unity, or do we reject them? Jesus prayed that we would all be one in Him. There is no room for prejudice and biased attitudes. Unconditional acceptance unleashes the scriptural dynamics for two or more to become one in Christ and to experience fellowship.

Every Believer Is Involved

In order to solve difficulties in a marriage, a husband and wife must decide that divorce is not an alternative. They discover how to get along and how to develop their love. In the same manner, within the body of Christ, each individual member must decide to accept other believers. With this attitude, believers can use scriptural principles to work through natural differences. By doing this, Christians can respond openly in their fellowship with one another.

Ideally fellowship involves every true believer. Realistically, though, we are limited by time and space. So our fellowship must begin with those believers with whom we have contact. How many people should be involved in forming a small group? A few people who have agreed to a common commitment can best experience fellowship. When this is done with as few as 2 or 3 (which qualifies for the unique promise of Christ's presence) or with as many as 13 (which is the size group Jesus modeled), we have an excellent beginning for a fellowship support group.

These small groups should function to supplement one's participation in a local church. But every church member can be spiritually enriched by small group fellowship.

Picture building a stone wall. A covenant of acceptance moves the stones into place for the construction. Peter describes believers in Christ as "living stones" (1 Peter 2:5). Paul portrays the church being built with Jesus Christ as the cornerstone and the apostles as the foundation (Eph. 2:20). As we make ourselves available, God, the Master Developer, fits us together in the structure.

The Lord's work can be likened to that of the stonemason of yesteryear. Even as those stonemasons fashioned the stones for the great castles of England, they could only lay three or four stones a day because of all the chiseling and cutting it took to fit the stones together compatibly.

In the same way it takes just as much chiseling, sandpapering (abrasive experiences), and cutting to get us to fit together in any group. Another analogy along this same line is that of the Mexican jumping bean. At the first sign of movement or abrasiveness, we tend to hop—usually away from the person. But being molded and fitly framed together is a requirement for any member of the body of Christ. So what must we do?

Availability

First, be available. Often when we feel uncomfortable with another believer, we withdraw. This can happen in small groups, local churches, Christian organizations, or even among seminary faculties. But Jesus said, "By this shall all men know that ye are My disciples, if ye have love one to another" (John 13:35, KJV). He wants us to love each other in the same way that He loves us (15:12).

How can we do this—especially with some people who seem so hard to love? The answer is we can't. But God can and will love others through us when we're really available. First, available to His indwelling presence and secondly, available to others physically, mentally, emotionally, and spiritually. This kind of availability costs. Jesus said, "If anyone wishes to come after Me, let him deny himself, and take up his cross daily, and follow Me" (Luke 9:23).

In his letter to the Galatian believers, Paul wrote about this subject. "I have been crucified with Christ; and it is no longer I who live, but Christ lives in me; and the life which I now live in the flesh I live by faith in the Son of God, who loved me, and delivered Himself up for me" (Gal. 2:20). To be in fellowship together in the brashness of personal offenses, prejudices, and irritations . . . I have to get out of the way and allow Christ to love that offending person through me. This "Love as I love you" is a far more vigorous involvement than the Old Testament standard of "Love your neighbor as yourself."

We are called to demonstrate the supernatural lifestyle of Christ Himself as He lives through our earthen vessels and displays His splendor. This kind of availability can be greatly enhanced by a fellowship group when it covenants together either verbally or nonverbally to unconditionally accept each other and pay the price of the cross of allowing Christ to live in and through them.

Acceptance and Forgiveness

Second, stick and grow where God plants you. When I try to do this I soon discover the living stones around me have that abrasive effect. They get on my nerves. I discover we're different. Sometimes I'm wrongfully hurt. So how can I stick? "And be kind to one another, tenderhearted, forgiving each other, just as God in Christ also has forgiven you" (Eph. 4:32). Love is the basic ingredient in the mortar that binds believers together. The mixture includes the water of the Holy Spirit and the powder of acceptance and forgiveness.

For the Apostle Peter, the matter of forgiveness raised a question. He asked the Lord, "How many times shall I forgive my brother when he sins against me? Up to seven times?" (Matt. 18:21, NIV) Jesus' answer changed Peter's perspective, "I do not say to you, up to seven times, but up to seventy times seven" (v. 22). In other words, Jesus was saying to forgive without limit.

This exchange between Peter and our Lord follows in context what Dr. Richard Halverson, pastor of the Fourth Presbyterian Church in Washington, D.C. calls "a cluster of three incredible fellowship promises." They are so fantastic that our spiritual computer goes haywire.

"Truly I say to you, whatever you shall bind on earth shall have been bound in heaven; and whatever you loose on earth shall have been loosed in heaven. Again I say to you, that if two of you agree on earth about anything that they may ask, it shall be done for them by My Father who is in heaven. For where two or three have gathered together in My name, there I am in their midst" (vv. 18-20). These verses are sandwiched on either side by Jesus' teaching on forgiveness.

Jesus taught that if we have a disagreement with someone, it is our responsibility to settle the dispute with that person. But if we've sinned against someone, we should still seek that person's forgiveness and make restitution wherever it is appropriate. Either way, we are to seek forgiveness. "Blessed are the peacemakers" (Matt. 5:9).

Our Lord amplified His answer to Peter with the Parable of the Unmerciful Servant (18:23-35). This servant would not forgive his fellow servant a small debt—even though his compassionate employer had forgiven him (the unmerciful servant) a huge sum. Fellow employees communicated the unfair employee's actions to the employer. The employer put the servant in prison. Jesus concluded the parable with these sober words: "So shall My heavenly Father also do to you, if each of you does not forgive his brother from your heart" (v. 35).

Forgiving Others Facilitates Fellowship

But where do we begin? We should start with those closest to us. God drove this truth home to me when I discovered as an adult that I still had some problems with my mother. While I was attending Bill Gothard's Institute in Basic Youth Conflicts seminar, I discovered that I had been harboring some ill feelings toward my mother. During the seminar, Bill asked the question, "Are there any particular kinds of people that you have difficulty in relating to? This can be a clue to unhealthy relationships. Our tendency is to reject all the people that come into our lives who remind us of a person we haven't forgiven."

As Bill continued, he described the process of cutting ourselves off from a whole segment of society. I realized that any time I got around a very strong, domineering type of woman I would smile and sneak away as quickly as possible. So as he suggested, I resurrected the hurts from my childhood. As each of these situations came to my mind, I forgave my mom. Afterward, I felt like an electric charge had buoyed me up. It was as though a lot of old carbon had been cleaned out of my spiritual exhaust system. The problem had been mine, not my mother's.

To forgive others is a requirement for maximum fellowship with God. But not only that, forgiveness is also a requirement for maximum fellowship with those closest to us.

Seeking Forgiveness Facilitates Fellowship

Some years ago I realized that I had offended my oldest son and needed to seek his forgiveness. I had been too domineering in our relationship. As a result, he often behaved in a rebellious way. When I finally realized that his actions were a response to my domineering attitude, I asked the Lord to forgive me. Then I called Randy, who was attending a college away from home, to seek his forgiveness. After we exchanged greetings and talked about the weather, I explained that my bossy attitude toward him had been wrong.

"I really feel bad about it," I said. "I want to ask if you would forgive me."

He answered, "Yes, Dad, I forgive you—and Dad?"

"Yes, Randy?"

"You know I have been rebellious a lot of times too. Would you forgive me?"

"You bet!"

Immediately, our fellowship deepened. Although we were over 700 miles apart, we were spiritually united by a bond that enabled us both to grow together. Through the years, our relationship has continued to grow.

Three of the hardest words to say are "I was wrong."

But these words and a repentant attitude seeking forgiveness from another form a mortar of love that will hold us together in fellowship.

Our Enemy

When Nehemiah led God's people in rebuilding the broken-down wall around Jerusalem, many skeptics and enemies opposed him. Likewise, as we seek to build solid relationships for God's glory, we are opposed. We have an enemy. Satan does not want us to live together harmoniously. To divide and conquer us, he uses a dangerous weapon—the fiery darts of imagined wrongs. In this subtle way, Satan tries to influence our lives through our thoughts.

The wall of acceptance built through love and forgiveness will shield and protect us against wrong thoughts. " 'Let none of you imagine evil in your hearts against his neighbor; and love no false oath: for all these are things that I hate,' saith the Lord" (Zech. 8:17, KJV).

Wrong imaginations about another person often turn into judgments. The battleground is our mind and the attitudes we contrive there. Paul wrote to the Romans that we should "Accept the one who is weak in faith, but not for the purpose of passing judgment on his opinions" (Rom. 14:1). To do that, we must bring every thought into captivity to the obedience of Christ (2 Cor. 10:5).

As we allow the Holy Spirit to apply God's words to our thought processes, we will find the ability to be patient with one another in love. Also, we will realize our place in God's building as living stones holding up others as others also support us. This is the concept of the fellowship support group, providing stability and support for the Christian life.

Anything shared in confidence within a fellowship support group becomes privileged information. Those in the group should guard it as such. Just as an attorney with his client or a physician with his patient—the wall of acceptance should hold in any communications that are private or could be harmful.

More than 100 years ago poet Edwin Markham described building a wall of acceptance this way:

> He drew a circle and left me out,
> A heretic, a rebel, a thing to flout,
> But love and I had the wit to win,
> We drew a circle and took him in!

We must be willing to take the first step. If we forgive others, they will be more willing to take us in, forgive us. Fellowship will be encouraged. Taking that first step, however, requires purposeful action. Fellowship can never be encouraged without our effort to put others first. To make this effort we must view God, His will, and others as more important than ourselves.

THREE

More Important than Me

Picture a tightrope walker without a net. What do you think would be on his mind? Perhaps he's nervous and the thought of falling lingers in the back of his mind. Or—he could be a study in pure concentration and commitment. But in either case, a slip could mean total disaster and his audience would stand by helpless—unable to do anything to assist.

On the other hand, what if the tightrope walker had his audience below holding a safety net for him? Not only would the audience be actively involved in the process, but they would be cheering him on to greater heights, more daring stunts. Both he and the audience would reap greater benefits from such teamwork. Each would support the other. As the tightrope walker provided more entertainment for the audience, he could remain assured that those below would catch him in a fall.

Christians walking life's tightrope need other believers to hold their net, give them support. The best way to see this happen in our own lives is to hold somebody else's net. Our challenge as believers lies not only in walking our own rope, but in bearing someone else's burden (Gal. 6:2), holding *their* net.

Paul explained this principle. He taught the Philippians not to look at their own interests, but at the interests of others (Phil. 2:3-4). This principle confuses unbelievers. They automatically look out for "number one." Usually their jobs rank second. Then come their families and friends. God falls at the lower end of their priority lists, if He makes it at all.

Unfortunately, we as Christians often fail to readjust our priorities when we trust Christ. Or, if we do try to get our lives shipshape with God at the helm, it only lasts until the "new" wears off. Nearly every evangelical believer I know faces (or has faced) the priority problem. It becomes compounded when we start trying to serve the interests of others in God's family.

The Challenge

Several years ago Doug Coe, one of the men who helped disciple Charles Colson during the Watergate scandal, came to my hometown. He challenged a few of us to band together in fellowship for a specific purpose. Would we commit ourselves to meet weekly, to pray for the needs of our community, and to take the responsibility of Jesus Christ for our area?

Mr. Coe's challenge was dramatic and his personality sparkled with love for the Saviour. Still, I did not see how I could fit another weekly prayer meeting into my already crammed schedule. I rationalized. *Who was I to take on that kind of responsibility for others?*

After the meeting, I expressed my reluctance to Mr. Coe. I told him about my involvement in home Bible studies and one-to-one discipleship. I needed another meeting like Jimmy Carter needs a bigger smile.

Doug asked me to pray about it. Pray about praying? I didn't know what to tell him. The very next morning in my time alone with God, I read these words: "Do nothing out of selfish ambition or vain conceit, but in humility consider others better than yourselves" (Phil. 2:3, NIV).

I asked myself, *Am I looking only at my own interests instead of the interests of others?* Then I read verse 4: "Look not every man on his own things, but every man also on the things of others" (KJV).

After reading that verse, I knew the Lord had caught me off base again. I had been focusing on my needs instead of others' needs. In the same chapter, Paul alerts the Philippians that he will soon send Timothy to them. He tells them his reason for sending Timothy is because he knew the young man would care for their needs.

"For I have no man like-minded, who will naturally care for your state. For all seek their own, not the things which are Jesus Christ's" (vv. 20-21, KJV).

Timothy had the commitment and desire to take the responsibility for the spiritual well-being of the Philippians. Otherwise, Paul would not have sent him. It was obvious to me that God wanted me to put aside my own interests to take the responsibility of Jesus Christ in any area He might desire. I accepted Doug's challenge.

I want to be a seeker of the things of Jesus Christ. How about you? Are you so involved in your own activities, your own program, your own organization (perhaps even your church) that you aren't free to look around for the things of Jesus Christ? Participating in a fellowship support group helps you find the things of Christ. It gives you the motivation to grab hold of someone else's net. It can give you the support you need to be actively involved in seeking the things of Christ. With that support (like Doug Coe gave me) you will find yourself looking at the interests of others first and allowing them to help you in your interests. Together you will see more clearly the things of Jesus Christ. Support, teamwork, involvement.

How does a fellowship support group actually work? You may be in a group already or perhaps you would like to join a group that provides this kind of support for one another. In either case, here are three suggestions to strengthen the support in any group.

Help One Another Set Priorities

The Bible clearly teaches a specific order for our personal priorities. When the Pharisees asked Jesus, "What is the greatest of all commandments?" He answered from the Old Testament. "Thou shalt love the Lord thy God with all thy heart, and with all thy soul, and with all thy mind. This is the first and great commandment. And the second is like unto it, Thou shalt love thy neighbor as thyself" (Matt. 22:37-39, KJV).

Jesus also spoke to the priority issue in His Sermon on the Mount. Matthew records how He told the multitudes to keep first things first in their lives and they would not feel anxious. "But seek ye first the kingdom of God, and His righteousness; and all these things shall be added unto you" (6:33, KJV). They would not have to worry about their daily needs if they kept their priorities straight.

In both of these passages Jesus unfolds the top priority item for anyone's list. God! The Lord is to be first in the life of any believer. Every one of us would agree with that assertion. But what about "His righteousness"? How many of us really seek His character? Do we really want to be like Him? Seeking God's righteousness means allowing His character to be formed in us. We need support and encouragement to foster that desire in our lives. We need fellowship.

And what about your neighbor? Who is he anyway? Well, look around. Start with your spouse. The person you're married to is probably the closest neighbor you'll ever have. Loving that person closest to you becomes your second priority. Then come children and family responsibilities, such as being a parent with whom God would be well pleased. Career responsibilities and financial stewardship fall in place next because of their effect on the family. Responsible attitudes and care toward your immediate associates and friends likewise remains high on the priority ladder.

The pivotal issue involved in the priority question is the importance of keeping God first and constantly evaluating the things we do in His light. Too often we do not recognize the Good Samaritan opportunities in our own traffic patterns of life nor our need to love and pray for our enemies. Fellowship support groups can provide the motivational cornerstone for the building and maintenance of these priority relationships.

My primary support group, with whom I meet weekly, started with three other men. Our group focuses on two avenues of ministry: prayer and priorities. At the outset we agreed to help each other by praying together weekly. Next, we submitted ourselves to be held accountable by the others in the group for priorities, to know Christ, and to meet the responsibilities He gives us.

We spent the first four weeks with each member giving a priority inventory of his life. Next, each evaluated his relations with his wife, his children, his business associates, his friends, and his nearby neighbors. Each week one brother discussed his situation, the others asked questions, helped him evaluate from new perspectives, and then prayed for him.

The next week another one of us shared and so on, till each was so familiar with the others' priorities that we could move on to other areas. One key to the group's effectiveness has been this basic attitude of humility. Not only does each man seek to bear a transparent image to the others, but each has been willing to look continually to the others' needs and interests.

Bear One Another's Burdens

Bearing another's burden involves both sharing and caring. We must first be willing to share our hurts, problems, and needs with each other. Then we can respond with the genuine love of willing the best for one another. By becoming transparent to the others in the group, we encourage them to open up also. This means that when someone shares a real need, I cannot be a passive listener. Rather, I must be an active spiritual participant, willing to enter into that situation and prayerfully get under the burden.

Paul examines the concept of bearing someone else's burden in Galatians 6:2. His explanation will blow most of our spiritual socks off. Bearing someone else's burden means fulfilling the perfect law of Christ, that is, love! Loving one's neighbor means bearing their burdens!

This kind of love cannot be indifferent. It must weep with those who weep and rejoice with those who rejoice. It demands that we look objectively at the other person's need. Otherwise, we're only giving sympathy—not love. To become a sympathy-giver is like jumping into a pool of quicksand with the person who is already caught in the muck! Both are then caught in the mire because neither one has a firm grip on solid ground.

Instead, we need to empathize with the one in need as a person who knows how to handle the quicksand. If we keep one hand on the solid ground of God's Word, we can reach out with the other hand to pull the struggling person to safety. We can't help unless we get close. But we can't help if we lose our solid grip either.

The Word of God is the sure foundation which, when gripped firmly, will enable us to help with people's burdens.

Jesus prescribed this for our lives in Matthew 7:24-25. Preaching to the multitudes in His Sermon on the Mount, He said, "Therefore everyone who hears these words of Mine and puts them into practice is like a wise man who built his house on the rock. The rain came down, the streams rose, and the winds blew and beat against that house; yet it did not fall, because it had its foundation on the rock" (NIV). Jesus spoke the word of God and the Bible is *our rock!*

Meet One Another's Needs

One might ask if this is not the same as putting another's interests first or bearing one another's burdens. But it is not. It differs in that needs involve behavioral patterns and the circumstances which result from them.

Two kinds of needs emerge in group situations, felt needs and unfelt needs. The *felt need* is a problem area, a desire, or a situation recognized by the person who voices it. That is, the person sees that he has a need and shares it willingly with the group.

As the group continues to meet, to pray together, and to share priorities and burdens, other needs emerge. These are *unfelt needs*. That is, these are blind spots which all of us have but have not yet recognized. Often these may be pivotal needs which, when met, will stimulate the person to a greater spiritual growth.

Many times an unfelt need will emerge at early meetings, but most take time to discern. It takes a deeper knowledge of a person's priorities, interests, burdens, and lifestyle to perceive his unfelt needs. We need to "crawl into his skin" and look at life through his eyes.

As our fellowship deepens, we will be able to recognize, evaluate, and share what we have detected as a need in someone else's life. The more involved the group becomes in this process, the more edification will take place at all levels. The depth of a fellowship support group's growth is proportionate to the recognition of unfelt needs within the group.

However, at this deeper level fiery darts and flaming arrows begin to fly. If a fellowship group intends to stay intact, those involved must realize the source of discouragement. When God throws the spotlight on somebody else's needs, we naturally tend to withdraw. It's not our problem; why should we point it out?

That is Satan's lie. We either feel insecure ourselves, or we don't want to suffer the abrasiveness of working through that need. Why should we risk rejection when we don't really have to? The devil will fire again and again to discourage such deep edification. He hates spiritual growth!

Paul gives us a great illustration of what God does with His church when the believers in it are edified and growing. He compares believers to living stones in a building being fitted together (Eph. 2:21-22). A lot of chiseling and sandpapering is required for the stones to fit together, whether it is in a marriage or a fellowship support group. Our first reaction toward unpleasantness in a close relationship is to separate. But separation is not God's desire. Stones and mortar will never form a building if they separate. In the same way the sovereign God places us together so that we might meet one another's needs and grow. His desire is for us to become holy temples, buildings fashioned for His occupancy, fitly framed together.

The following excerpt from a personal letter illustrates God's spotlight on needs. It also demonstrates areas of tension where Satan could creep in and destroy the fellowship. It is from Glen McCaskey, a young business executive at Hilton Head Island, South Carolina. He wrote me not long after his first experience in a fellowship support group. After meeting with other men for several weeks in prayer, this is a portion of what he shared:

One thing I am realizing is the degree to which each one of us has an absolutely unique walk with the Lord, that we are indeed as different as our fingerprints and that even aspects of our belief are different. Fundamentally, we are all certainly on equal footing, but we see God doing different things. . . . And we trust Him in different ways depending on what He is revealing to us in our own lives. This is, of course, what the body of Christ is all about and the blessing of it, and I guess I am just starting to appreciate that in greater depth than before. I personally have to constantly fight a tendency to be controlling and I suspect that I had envisioned and wanted a greater cleaving together of the group than we have at this time. Somehow I want to "make" that happen on my timetable.

That letter illustrates the differences between individuals—differences we often don't realize until we are committed to a small group fellowship. But one common factor remains with all groups: When the group probes for unfelt needs, the "honeymoon" stage ends. When it survives the satanic onslaught inevitable in the process of recognizing and meeting those deep needs that people cannot recognize by themselves, it has made a move toward solid maturity. If we faithfully meet one another's needs, God has promised to take us on to maturity.

Needs may be physical or financial. Most often, however, they are spiritual and can be met through some combination of two avenues of communication. On occasion it is best to speak directly to the person involved. We are told by Paul, "Instead, speaking the truth in love, we will in all things grow up into Him who is the Head, that is, Christ" (Eph. 4:15, NIV). The other avenue is less direct, but often more effective. It is speaking to God on behalf of that person, "And pray in the Spirit on all occasions with all kinds of prayers and requests" (6:18, NIV).

Summing Up

We have seen three principles which deal with recognizing that in God's program revealed in the Bible, other people should be more important to me than myself. Helping one another keep personal priorities in order, bearing the burden of another person, and helping to meet that person's needs should concern us more than our own needs and interests.

All three of these principles are well illustrated in the story Jesus told in Mark 2. When four people brought their lame friend to Jesus, they were literally bearing his burden, carrying him to the One who could meet his needs. As they tore open a hole in the roof and lowered their friend to Jesus, He responded to their faith and healed their friend. "Son," He said, "thy sins be forgiven thee" (Mark 2:5, KJV). The spiritual need outweighed the physical, but He also met the physical need.

Supporting one another means holding the stretcher and exercising faith on behalf of another person. Sometimes, we may be required to put ourselves humbly on the stretcher and let others exercise their faith on our behalf.

Once a group of believers has learned to put others first, what comes next? How may a group go on to further growth, further encouragement?

FOUR

What's the Syllabus for Growth?

The speaker was saying, "Just go through this syllabus with some men from your church and they will have been discipled. They in turn can take 6 to 12 men through this notebook and they also will have been discipled. The Scripture basis is 2 Timothy 2:2: 'And the things you have heard me say in the presence of many witnesses entrust to reliable men who will also be qualified to teach others'" (NIV).

As this man addressed the crowd, I asked myself, *Is this discipleship? Take some men through a notebook and they have been discipled?*

Being a disciple of Jesus Christ is a lifetime process of believing and following the Lord, not a study project. A fellowship support group can help this process because none of us can reach maturity in Christ by ourselves.

If we are to help one another, we need a clear picture of God's objective for us and *His syllabus* for our spiritual growth. If we understand what God is doing, then we can cooperate with Him as wise master builders. As the psalmist wrote, "Unless the Lord builds the house, they labor in vain who build it" (Ps. 127:1). Only God can make a man or woman godly. What is His ultimate objective for us individually? He desires that we glorify Him by becoming like Jesus. What then is His syllabus for generating this maturing process? It is all of life.

The Apostle Paul conveyed this same message to the Christians in Rome: "And we know that in all things God works for the good of those who love Him, who have been called according to His purpose. For those God foreknew He also predestined to be conformed to the likeness of His Son" (Rom. 8:28-29, NIV).

God's Love and Our Need

In order to visualize this process, let's construct an illustration that we will call "God's Perspective for Life." We begin with a person as he starts down the highway of life. The jagged line represents the ups and downs in life. We all have peaks and valleys, victories and defeats, problems and prosperities. The jagged line illustrates these variables. As God looks at people on this highway of life He might ask, "What is My first desire for each person?"

God loves us and has sent His Son to die on the cross so that we might have a relationship with Him. "For God so loved the world that He gave His one and only Son, that whoever believes in Him shall not perish but have eternal life. For God did not send His Son into the world to condemn the world, but to save the world through Him" (John 3:16-17, NIV).

God is not willing that any should perish, but that all people should come to repentance (2 Peter 3:9). Jesus told Nicodemus that he needed to be born again. God's first desire for us is that we know Him, that we be born into His spiritual family. Paul wrote that God "Desires all men to be saved and to come to the knowledge of the truth. For there is one God, and one Mediator also between God and men, the man Christ Jesus, who gave Himself as a ransom for all" (1 Tim. 2:4-6). Christ died for all people, especially those who believe (1 Tim. 4:10).

God, in love, has made His decision to have a relationship with us. However, He knows that there is not a person on earth who is perfect (Rom. 3:23). To be related to the perfect God we must either achieve perfection or have it given to us. He has made provision for this in the death of His Son on the cross. So, there are two constants in this illustration: God's love and our need.

When I meet someone new and I want to help that person, I must first discern his spiritual need. Is he a Christian? If not, then I need to love that person with God's love and encourage him to believe in Jesus Christ. The Scriptures liken this process to the growing of a crop: One plants, another waters, but God gives the increase (1 Cor. 3:6). If God uses me to move someone closer to Him, then I have given that person the most help I can give.

After someone has received Christ, he continues down the highway of life with all of its ups and downs. Often outward changes are not readily apparent. It may take growth and time before outward signs of God's Holy Spirit appear. However, God has a destination for everyone who has accepted Christ and those outward signs are part of the plan. God desires the same end for every individual who has a relationship with Him.

God's Bull's-eye for Us

God's bull's-eye is conformity to the image of Christ. God desires that each person who knows Him might become a mature individual just like Christ. Yet He also wants each person to retain his individual distinctiveness and personality. The drive to help others achieve this goal was expressed by Paul when he wrote, "My children, with whom I am again in labor until Christ is formed in you" (Gal. 4:19). "We proclaim Him, admonishing every man and teaching every man with all wisdom, that we may present every man complete in Christ. And for this purpose also I labor, striving according to His power, which mightily works within me" (Col. 1:28-29). Likewise, Paul said that his primary personal quest in life was to know Him (Phil. 3:10).

What is involved in the process of discipleship? It involves taking the next step or steps that God wants us to take toward our own spiritual maturity. Each day we need to fix our attention on Christ and progress toward Him.

In the Book of Hebrews we read:

Therefore, since we are surrounded by such a great cloud of witnesses, let us throw off everything that hinders and the sin that so easily entangles, and let us run with perseverance the race marked out for us. Let us fix our eyes on Jesus, the Author and Perfecter of our faith, who for the joy set before Him endured the cross, scorning its shame, and sat down at the right hand of the throne of God. Consider Him who endured such opposition from sinful men, so that you will not grow weary and lose heart (Heb. 12:1-3, NIV).

Help Each Other Grow

We do not travel the road of life alone. We're involved with our spouses, our children, our fellowship support groups, and in the broadest sense with all those who know Christ. We are all people in process. We have not arrived at full maturity and will not until we graduate from this life. Then we will be like Him for we will see Him as He is (1 John 3:2).

In the meantime we should be on the journey, growing together to be more like Him. It is together that we can grow. To be used by God in discipling another means being willing to reach out to help that person take the next step toward his own spiritual maturity.

The corporate responsibility of believers for one another is well described by the Apostle Paul:

It was He who gave some to be apostles, some to be prophets, some to be evangelists, and some to be pastors and teachers, to prepare God's people for works of service, so that the body of Christ may be built up until we all reach unity in the faith and in the knowledge of the Son of God and become mature, attaining to the whole measure of the fullness of Christ. Then we will no longer be infants, tossed back and forth by the waves, and blown here and there by every wind of teaching and by the cunning and craftiness of men in their deceitful scheming. Instead, speaking the truth in love, we will in all things grow up into Him who is the Head, that is, Christ. From Him the whole body, joined and held together by every supporting ligament, grows and builds itself up in love, as each part does its work (Eph. 4:11-16, NIV).

The body builds itself up in the maturity of Christ. In a fellowship support group the members have the opportunity to give that helping hand to their fellow group members. God uses everything that comes into our lives to help us mature (Rom. 8:28). By understanding this process, we can respond in a godly way to the crisis situations that arise. In my own life when there is a lesson that I need to learn, I find that the runners come over the hill from all directions. This is illustrated by the arrows below:

One of those runners might come as I hear God's Word preached or shared by someone else. Another might come as I read the Word on my own. Still another might come from the responses of people around me or by circumstances. I need to be looking constantly for the common denominator for the instructions of life. That common denominator will tell me what I need to be learning from my relationships, circumstances, and situations. Real life, all of it, is God's school of learning for us.

There are also two constants on this other side of the cross: God's love and our need. Anyone I meet who is a believer I know God loves and I want to let Him love the believer through me. I also know this person has needs, because we're all needy. If God gives me a relationship with this person then I should be available to help him grow in his own spiritual maturity.

A Personal Example

I met with a man recently who asked for spiritual help. Since

I am not a spiritual soothsayer, I asked him questions about the four dynamics which I have found necessary to keep Christ at the center of my life: the Word of God, prayer, fellowship, and witnessing. He then expressed that his need related to the Bible, being able to apply it in his life. He told me several ways this need had been brought to his awareness. I read his feelings as he described the runners coming over the hill showing him his need. We have now embarked on projects together to encourage one another in Scripture memory and personal application.

In other words, I let him tell me what he felt the next step was that he should take toward his own maturity in Christ. Now I am encouraging and helping him to take that step and at the same time I am learning from him. We are two people on the journey together to know Christ. We help each other in Christian fellowship.

As Dr. Richard C. Halverson, pastor of the Fourth Presbyterian Church in Washington, D.C. wrote in his devotional letter, *Perspective* (Concern Ministries, Inc., February 28, 1979):

It's not what happens to you that makes the difference. . . . It's what happens in you! What happens to you is destructive only in terms of what you allow to happen in you. To put it another way—you may not be able to prevent what is done to you . . . but you can decide how you take it. You may allow circumstances to embitter you—make you vindictive, jealous, envious. . . . But when you do, you release emotions in your system which trigger body chemistry and poison you. Or you may take circumstances in stride in the confidence that your life is ordered of the Lord and that He will use everything that happens to you for your own good. Growing in grace and in the knowledge of Jesus Christ works this way. . . . The school of the Spirit involves suffering, pain, failure, sin. . . . All of which are recycled by the grace of God into maturity. Don't resent what happens to you. . . . Rejoice in the knowledge that God is working for your benefit in whatever happens. We know that God works in everything for good to them who love Him who are called according to His purpose (Rom. 8:28).

God can use anything to make someone beautiful. This is the same principle of the jagged grain of sand in the oyster shell which develops into a pearl. Jesus preached this precept from Isaiah 61:1-3 when He began His public ministry (compare with Luke 4:18-19).

The Spirit of the Lord God is upon me, because the Lord has anointed me to bring good news to the afflicted; He has sent me to bind up the broken-hearted, to proclaim liberty to captives, and freedom to prisoners; to proclaim the favorable year of the Lord, and the day of vengeance of our God; to comfort all who mourn, to grant those who mourn in Zion, giving them a garland instead of ashes, the oil of gladness instead of mourning, the mantle of praise instead of a spirit of fainting. So they will be called oaks of righteousness, the planting of the Lord, that He may be glorified.

The syllabus for growth toward maturity in Christ is *all of life*. What an opportunity we have in a small group situation to help others and likewise see ourselves grow in the constant process of discipleship. In that very process, as we view the message of Romans 8:28, one issue stands above all. We must learn to do things *God's* way.

FIVE

I'll Do It His Way

During the late 1960s Frank Sinatra and Elvis Presley popularized Paul Anka's song, "I'll Do It My Way." Sinatra's booming voice and Presley's mass appeal not only sold millions of records but also helped to spread a philosophy which has literally taken over as the accepted view for today's society. The watchword has become "do your own thing," and it finds its expression in phrases like "assert yourself," "intimidate others and win," "look after yourself first," or "if it feels good, do it." All of these are just variations of the first. Our sinful human nature expresses itself with these words: "I'll do it *my* way!"

But that philosophy opposes God's way. In Gethsemane just before His own crucifixion Christ prayed, "Not My will, but *Thine* be done" (Luke 22:42, italics added). Christ's desire was to please His Father. His attitude demonstrated the ultimate in submission.

Paul reiterated this attitude: "So we make it our goal to please Him" (2 Cor. 5:9, NIV). Again, God's will, not ours, is seen as of ultimate importance. This point is made again in verse 15, "And He died for all, that those who live should no longer live for themselves but for Him who died for them and was raised again" (NIV). So the orientation of our lives should be as Christ's, "So that in everything *He* might have the supremacy" (Col. 1:18, NIV).

Yielding to God

God's way is submission: first to Christ, then to one another. But the worldly attitude "my way" has spilled over onto Christians. The problem is, if we see a spiritual superstar we might submit to him. We want to pick and choose to whom we will spiritually submit, usually based on that person's status, charisma, or authority.

Our basis of submission should be the Lord, not the popularity of the one to whom we're submitting. Usually we submit to our banker, attorney, or physician before we submit to a brother or sister in Christ. We also say we submit to the invisible God—but then we reject Him when He speaks to us through another person.

One scriptural example of this is found in the discourses between Jesus and the Pharisees. The Pharisees claimed that Jesus' witness was not true. They wanted to know who He really was. Jesus responded that He is the Son of God. "Jesus said to them, 'Truly, truly, I say to you, before Abraham was born, I AM.' Therefore they picked up stones to throw at Him; but Jesus hid Himself, and went out of the temple" (John 8:58-59).

Again, consider Jesus' model of submission. He made Himself of no reputation and as a man became obedient to His Father even to death (Phil. 2:8). Jesus taught His disciples that even He, the Son of man, came to serve and to give His life as a ransom for many. And we're to do the same—serving and submitting to others. This procedure, according to the Scriptures, spurs us on to love and good deeds.

"And let us consider how to stimulate one another to love and good deeds, not forsaking our own assembling together, as is the habit of some, but encouraging one another; and all the more, as you see the day drawing near" (Heb. 10:24-25).

Submission is the dynamic which augments cooperation. It begins in a heart yielded to God's authority. Jesus said, "But do not be called Rabbi; for One is your Teacher, and you are all brothers. And do not call anyone on earth your father; for One is your Father, He who is in heaven. And do not be called leaders; for One is your Leader, that is, Christ. But the greatest among you shall be your servant. And whoever exalts himself shall be humbled; and whoever humbles himself shall be exalted" (Matt. 23:8-12).

As we truly yield to God from our hearts, we will be submissive to one another. In fact, Paul said this vertical submission is the key to submission on the horizontal level. "Submit to one another out of reverence for Christ" (Eph. 5:21, NIV).

The Coordinated Body of Christ

One of the most heart-rending scenes is a spastic person attempting to move down the street. Each arm going a different direction, head bobbing back and forth, knees turned inward and one foot dragging. All too often the body of Jesus Christ on earth looks spastic, with each member doing what is right in his own eyes. Instead, God wants us to look like an Olympic athlete. Visualize a high-hurdler, his arms and legs moving in picture-perfect synchronization as he leaps each barrier with all the skill of a champion, all the grace of a ballet dancer. Moving in graceful coordination, each member of the body becomes trained to submit to its adjoining members so that all move in unified obedience to the head. This is the opposite of the "one-upmanship" being promoted from all angles. God's way is cooperation, not competition.

We are told to be submissive one to another, not to be

authorities one to another. I shouldn't try to superimpose my authority on another. This submission should be implemented from the inside out, not from the outside in. We're all to be brothers and sisters, not bosses.

The first time I experienced real submission with my fellowship support group it was scary. We had been meeting together weekly for about seven years before I was finally willing to trust my brothers for God's direction and to know the mind of Christ (1 Cor. 2:16). Some other men had asked me to assume a responsibility which could mean extended time outside of our own community and I wanted to do it. I felt God wanted me to do it, but a major decision that could involve a lot of time meant I should submit the proposition to my prayer partners. They asked me a lot of pertinent, probing questions and said they would like to consider it for a week or two and then discuss it again. In that interim I had to search my own soul—what would I do if they said no?

A few days later my wife asked, "What will you do if they say no?" If they said no, then I wouldn't do it. I would take it as God's sign that He was either saying "No, don't do it at all," or "Wait until a later time." This would not be a natural reaction for me. As a business entrepreneur and president of my own company, I was not accustomed to getting direction from others—especially for my personal life.

In due time we met and the group members expressed their thinking. In my heart I believed their opinions would be my divine guidance. When it was all finished there was a unanimous unity that I should proceed with my plans. What freedom and liberty has resulted from that submission!

James wrote:

> But prove yourselves doers of the Word, and not merely hearers who delude themselves. For if any one is a hearer of the Word and not a doer, he is

like a man who looks at his natural face in a mirror; for once he has looked at himself and gone away, he has immediately forgotten what kind of person he was. But one who looks intently at the perfect law, the law of liberty, and abides by it, not having become a forgetful hearer but an effectual doer, this man shall be blessed in what he does" (James 1:22-25).

It is incomprehensible that through submission comes freedom, but isn't this divine economics? "He who loves his life loses it; and he who hates his life in this world shall keep it to life eternal" (John 12:25).

Seldom is this dynamic of submission really experienced in the body of Christ. Either we do not take time to be intimately involved with others, or we are not willing to take the risk of trusting others for spiritual guidance. But when we as the body of Christ learn to submit we will be like the graceful high-hurdler instead of the spastic man.

Active Submission

Another example of submission in a major decision involved the move of our family from Wichita, Kansas to Dallas, Texas. We had lived in Wichita for nine years, seven of which I had been involved in weekly prayer with the same fellowship support group. My involvement in my local church and with the seven men with whom I had an in-depth discipling relationship seemed to be winding down. I wondered if the experience of the men in my discipleship group might not be similar to that of the believers mentioned in Acts 9:31 after Paul left them: "So the church throughout all Judea and Galilee and Samaria enjoyed peace, being built up; and, going on in the fear of the Lord and in the comfort of the Holy Spirit, it continued to increase."

The Lord seemed to be leading us to relocate because of increased business and ministry activities outside of the Kansas community. But what would the brothers say? I presented the pros and cons for the move, answered their questions, and awaited their decision.

Several weeks later we met again to discuss this matter. It was not an easy wait for me, even though I was trusting them for God's will. When we met, each man expressed the opinion that it was God's will that we move. The group was unanimous. What freedom and liberty I experienced from this submission. It was suggested that I report back from time to time on what God would do. This reporting back has been a continuing source of strength and prayer support since our relocation.

Solution to Selfishness

The Book of Judges records Israel's experience in periodically submitting to God through others. When they submitted, they were blessed. When they didn't submit, they had big problems. The last verse of the Book of Judges analyzes the problem we face when we do not submit to one another out of our reverence for God. "In those days there was no king in Israel: every man did that which was right in his own eyes" (Judges 21:25, KJV).

Sound familiar? The same attitude prevails today. Submission is scoffed at by most people as "old fashioned"—whether it be in the home or in society. The biggest problem fostered by the "do-it-my-way" philosophy has been the growth of rampant immorality. The moral fiber of our nation hangs in the balance. As evangelical Christians teeter on the rim, threatening to become more like the world, it becomes apparent that something must be done to cure us of this selfish attitude. Three answers immediately come to mind.

First, as Francis Schaeffer has exclaimed, we must return

to "biblical absolutes" (From "How Should We Then Live?" Seminar, Dallas, February, 1977). That is, we must begin to regard the Bible's answers as God's, and follow its design. Second, we must learn the biblical pattern of submission and follow it. Love follows submission and when such an attitude is apparent among believers, God will be well-pleased. Third, we need a healthy dose of revival. Fellowship support groups can help stimulate just such a revival. To see such a moving of God's Spirit, we must learn to believe God.

SIX

What's the Program, Lord?

Jesus' words were sometimes misunderstood by His listeners. Such was the case when He told the crowd, "Do not work for the food which perishes, but for the food which endures to eternal life" (John 6:27). They responded, "What shall we do, that we may work the works of God?" (v. 28) Jesus answered with a new spiritual principle. "This is the work of God, that you believe in Him whom He has sent" (v. 29).

You can imagine what the people's reaction was. "But wait a minute, Lord! Isn't there some organization that we must join? Aren't we supposed to do a great work for You? Certainly, Lord, You want us to be doing something for somebody else! Surely there is *something* we must *do* if we're to inherit eternal life!" But Jesus said if we want to labor for that which does not perish, then our labor is to *believe* God and His Son, Jesus Christ.

The Neglected Principle

Perhaps the most neglected principle of Christian fellowship is believing God *together*. When we pray, God is listening. In fact, according to Romans 8:26 when we truly yearn Godward in our heart, the Holy Spirit intercedes for us and brings our requests before Him.

Believing prayer is the ultimate in the art of communication. All 16 of the saints mentioned in Hebrews 11 are included because they had faith. Oh, that we might come together and truly believe God is the Lord! That we might believe He is who He says He is! That we might believe He will indeed fulfill every word and promise He has made! Jesus says that for these things to become real in our lives we must believe Him. "And without faith it is impossible to please Him, for he who comes to God must believe that He is, and that He is a rewarder of those who seek Him" (Heb. 11:6).

So often when we gather, our fellowship meetings turn to "doing." They become committee meetings, programming what we might do for God. Yet what God desires is that we believe Him, thereby enabling Him to do for us and through us what He desires.

Unfortunately, it is usually easier for us to act than to pray. Peter had this problem too (Luke 22:40-51; John 18:10). The Lord had asked Peter to watch and pray with Him, but Peter and the other apostles fell asleep. Then when the Jews came to arrest Jesus, Peter drew his sword and cut off the right ear of the high priest's slave. The Lord patched everything up (He healed the man's ear), and used it as an object lesson. Those who live by the sword will perish by the sword (Matt. 26:52).

This example reminds us that it is easier to be physically rather than spiritually active. Our Lord had called on Peter to pray and He calls on us for the same thing. When a few people come together in prayer and believe God, much is accomplished. The effectiveness of prayer for believers is even greater now, because Jesus intercedes for us, pleading our case and giving us strength.

Prayer That Works

In my prayer group in Wichita, Kansas we were concerned for the youth of our city. In the late 60s it seemed that this area of our community was especially hurting. Several churches were without youth ministers. One in particular was Eastminster Presbyterian Church. When our fellowship group realized that this church body was looking for a youth minister, we prayed for them, according to the directions of the Lord. "The harvest is plentiful, but the workers are few. Therefore beseech the Lord of the harvest to send out workers into His harvest" (Matt. 9:37-38). We asked God to raise up His man for this position.

In due time, Eastminster Presbyterian Church employed a man who subsequently developed a strong youth program there. In fact, last year I was talking to a young fellow who came out of this man's ministry. He told me that today there are at least seven men who are in vocational Christian work from that church's youth group.

Young Life and Youth for Christ were also without leaders in Wichita. Our fellowship group prayed the same prayer, asking God to send His workers. Over a period of time, God answered by sending capable leaders.

One young man, Tom Rozof, appeared in our city and gathered a nucleus of young people around him. When *Time* magazine reported on the national "Jesus Movement," Wichita was named as a place of intense activity. Many of these fine young people have become mature servants of Christ.

Another prayer was answered when one of the downtown churches employed a young lady as youth leader. She moved to Wichita and started a singing group of seven boys and girls. The group, which grew to more than 300 members, called themselves "All God's Children." This sparked the young people's interest so much that youth singing groups sprang up in churches all over our community.

What we had viewed as a spiritual weak spot in our community became one of our strengths. What made the difference? God—for He is pleased to move mountains when a few people believe Him and pray according to His directions. We learned that as we believe God, even though our faith is as small as a mustard seed, He answers. Generally He meets our needs through other people. So as we prepare to pray with others, we should share what we know in order to bring needs before God.

When David became king and brought the Ark of the Covenant back to Jerusalem, he appointed priests to watch over it. He gave the priests three tasks: make petitions, give thanks, and praise the Lord (1 Chron. 16:8-9). Isn't it amazing that our sovereign God, the Creator of heaven and earth, wants us not only to give thanks and praise to Him, but also to make petitions to Him? He wants us to depend on Him.

Learning to depend on Him means learning to exercise our faith. Nothing is too small to bring before God. According to Paul, we should "Be anxious for nothing, but in everything by prayer and supplication with thanksgiving let your requests be made known to God. And the peace of God, which surpasses all comprehension, shall guard your hearts and your minds in Christ Jesus" (Phil. 4:6-7).

A House in the Ghetto

Another spiritual need which our fellowship group brought to the Lord concerned the black community in Wichita. Since there was very little spiritual activity in the ghetto section of our city, we made this a target of prayer. It wasn't too long before we heard about some young people from the Mennonite colleges in the small towns nearby. They had started several dozen youth clubs among the blacks and Mexican-Americans in Wichita's ghettos. The youth clubs, which met on Saturday mornings, combined athletics and Bible studies. The work had begun—because workers appeared.

By a series of events, Dr. Keith Phillips, president of World Impact, and Al Ewert, his key man in charge, came to one of our weekly prayer sessions. They shared with us what was happening in their ministry. Their biblical basis came from 1 John 3:18, "Little children, let us not love with word or with tongue, but in deed and truth."

Then one of our group members asked, "What is your greatest need right now?" Dr. Phillips replied that they needed a house in the ghetto. They had a vision of young people living there to penetrate the area for Christ. They hoped that demonstrating God's love by distributing food and meeting practical needs would result in God raising up black disciples for Christ. But they needed a facility, for which they had no money. We then joined together in prayer and asked God to provide such a house *before* Dr. Phillips left town.

After prayer, Dr. Phillips told us that he was scheduled to leave town the next day at 5 P.M. For almost eight months he had been looking for a house—but with no success. He was scheduled to meet with several pastors before he left Wichita. He hoped to work something out with one of them.

But the pastors didn't respond. However, a lady who wasn't supposed to be at the meeting had come. When she heard about the ministry and the need for a house, she approached Dr. Phillips. "We have a house located right in the heart of the ghetto. We have been praying about someone using it. Do you think it would be satisfactory?" she asked.

Praise the Lord! God not only provided *that* house, but subsequently the one next door also. And one of the churches represented at the meeting paid all the utility bills. The work has developed so much that there are several young black men and women now serving on the World Impact staff or voluntarily associated with it.

Agreeing to Believe

But all of this should not be strange to us. Jesus said that if two or three agree in prayer and really believe God, He will answer. "Again, I tell you that if two of you on earth agree about anything you asked for, it will be done for you by My Father in heaven" (Matt. 18:19, NIV).

But what does it mean to "agree"? As I understand it, it has a different connotation than just deciding on something and then, through prayer, trying to gain God's approval. Instead, it refers to those times when we are so unified with God and with each other that we can see a situation from His viewpoint. Then when we bring it before Him in prayer—it is done. This kind of oneness doesn't happen automatically, but requires believing.

Of course, before we agree together about something, we should try to discern God's will in the matter. The safest criteria for knowing God's will is to know God's Word. God's will is *never* contrary to His Word. The better we know His Word, the clearer His plan for us will be. Our attitude becomes "Your will not mine."

When believers are individually in spiritual tune with the Father and with each other, things happen. Answered prayers can come like lightning bolts in an electrical storm. Or the answers may be even slower, like an acorn gradually becoming an oak. But be assured that when two believers agree in harmony with God's will, God has promised to answer.

Facts That Build Faith

As a step toward greater belief, consider these "facts for faith" and their appropriation. The Bible is the most helpful essential in truly believing God because generally it is much more a "fact" book than a "why" book. Accepting and appropriating relevant facts from God can turn the tide in our struggle for belief. Abraham "staggered not at the promise of God through unbelief; but was strong in faith, giving glory to God" (Rom. 4:20, KJV).

In another instance, Moses expressed great doubt about being chosen to lead the Israelites. "Behold, I am going to the sons of Israel, and I shall say to them, 'The God of your fathers has sent me to you.' Now they may say to me, 'What is His name?' What shall I say to them?" (Ex. 3:13)

God answered with the great fact of His incomprehensible identity: " 'I AM WHO I AM'; and He said, 'Thus you shall say to the sons of Israel, "I AM has sent me to you." ' And God, furthermore, said to Moses, 'Thus you shall say to the sons of Israel, "The Lord, the God of your fathers, the God of Abraham, the God of Isaac, and the God of Jacob, has sent me to you." This is My name forever, and this is My memorial-name to all generations' " (vv. 14-15). This laid the foundation for the last 40 years of Moses' life. He became God's representative and he led the Israelites triumphantly out of the Pharaoh's clutches. He believed I AM!

As Charles Trumbull told a story in his book, *Victory in Christ,* he related the circumstances that revolutionized the life of one of the best-known Christian ministers of Great Britain. God made this man a tower of strength for 45 years.

"It was back in 1874 that a young Church of England vicar, the Rev. J. W. Webb-Peploe, with his wife, went to a seashore place with their youngest child, then a year old. At this place Mr. Webb-Peploe met Sir Arthur Blackwood, and when the older man learned the calling of the younger, he held his hand tightly as he asked, 'Have you got "rest"? '

" 'Yes, I hope so,' replied the young minister.

" 'What do you mean by that?' came the further question.

" 'That my sins are all forgiven through the blood of Jesus Christ, and that He will take me home to heaven when I die.'

" 'Yes, but what about the time between? Have you rest in all your work as a clergyman, and in your parish troubles?'

" 'No, I wish I had,' said the young minister honestly.

" 'I want the same,' said Sir Arthur, 'and today the great Oxford Convention begins.' (The Oxford Convention was the forerunner of the Keswick Convention.) 'Mrs. Trotter is going to write to me every day an account of the meetings; you and I can meet and pray that God will give us the blessing of the rest of faith which they are going to speak of there. God is not confined to Oxford.'

"For three days the two men met together, and then Mr. Webb-Peploe's little child was suddenly taken away by the heavenly Father. The young earthly father took the little body home, and reached there much wounded in feeling through contact with people who did not understand his circumstances. After the funeral, he began to prepare a sermon to preach to his people. He took for his text the passage found in the lesson for the day, 2 Corinthians 12:9, KJV—'My grace is sufficient for thee.' He spent some two hours in working on the sermon, and then he said to himself: 'It is not true; I do not find it sufficient under this heavy trouble that has befallen me.' And his heart cried out to God to make His grace sufficient for his hour of sore need and crushing sorrow.

"As he wiped the tears away from his eyes, he glanced up and saw over his study table an illuminated text-card that his mother had given him. The words read, 'My grace is sufficient for thee,' the word *is* being in bold type and in a different color from all the other words in the text. And Prebendary Webb-Peploe said 40 years later, as he told the incident, that he seemed to hear a voice saying to him: 'You fool, how dare you ask God to make what is? Believe His Word. Get up and trust Him, and you will find it true at every point.' He took God at His word, he believed the fact, and his life was revolutionized. He entered into such an experience of rest and peace, such trust in a sufficient Saviour, as he never before had dreamed could be possible. Within a month the governess in the family said to Mrs. Webb-Peploe, 'The farmers are remarking how much changed the vicar is: he does not seem fretful any more, but seems to be quiet and gentle about everything.' And from that day to this, now 45 years later, many another has praised God that the life of this minister of the Gospel is a testimony to the sufficiency of the grace which God declares is a fact" (taken from copyrighted material used by permission of the Christian Literature Crusade, Fort Washington, Pa. 19034, pp. 77-80).

The Secret of Victory

The secret of victory is not praying, but praising—not asking, but thanking. The writer of the Book of Hebrews reminds us of the past failure of God's people:

But the message they heard was of no value to them, because those who heard did not combine it with faith. Now we who have believed enter that rest, just as God has said, "So I declared on oath in My anger, 'They shall never enter My rest.' "

It still remains that some will enter that rest, and those who formerly had the Gospel preached to them did not go in, because of their disobedience. Therefore God again set a certain day, calling it Today, when a long time later He spoke through David, as was said before: "Today, if you hear His voice, do not harden your hearts."

There remains, then, a Sabbath-rest for the people of God; for anyone who enters God's rest also rests from his own work, just as God did from His. Let us, therefore, make every effort to enter that rest, so that no one will fall by following their example of disobedience (Heb. 4:2b-3, 6-7, 9-11, NIV).

As we endeavor to believe God, we experience spiritual growth. But that most fundamental step doesn't end the process. God has given every believer certain responsibilities within the body of Christ to help build it up, to help others grow.

SEVEN

What Can
I Bring
to the Party?

When we are born the first time, certain qualities are missing because we are born with a sin nature. For me, my sense of time was either left out or was very weak. I tend to procrastinate and have always been poor in time management.

However, when we are born again the Lord starts building in us what was left out the first time. How can I get more done in less time? How can I effectively use each opportunity? This quest to overcome my own weakness has led me to an exciting discovery.

The springboard for this discovery was this verse: "For through the grace given to me I say to every man among you not to think more highly of himself than he ought to think; but to think so as to have sound judgment, as God has allotted to each a measure of faith" (Rom. 12:3). In verse 6 we read, "And since we have gifts that differ according to the grace given to us, let each exercise them accordingly: if prophecy, according to the proportion of his faith."

In evaluating ways that I might be used most by God, I discovered the subject of spiritual gifts. Peter said that "Each one should use whatever gift he has received to serve others, faithfully administering God's grace in its various forms" (1 Peter 4:10, NIV).

Paul told the believers at Corinth, "Now concerning spiritual gifts, brethren, I do not want you to be unaware" (1 Cor. 12:1). Generally, believers in Christ are spiritually ignorant concerning their gifts. Members of a fellowship support group can serve one another by identifying and utilizing missing gifts.

How Do Spiritual Gifts Differ from Natural Abilities?

When we are born physically, we receive a unique combination of talents, abilities, and weaknesses. Our individual physical and personality traits are a gift from God. In the light of seeing God as our Creator, Paul asked three good questions to prevent strife: "What are you so puffed up about? What do you have that God hasn't given you? And if all you have is from God, why act as though you are so great, and as though you have accomplished something on your own" (1 Cor. 4:7, LB).

Paul asked the Corinthians to realize that all they were, both physically and spiritually, was a result of God's creating them and bringing them to Himself in salvation. Like the Corinthians, we need to thank God for making us and accept ourselves the way we are.

When we are born again, we receive spiritual characteristics. We become new creatures (2 Cor. 5:17), and new members of the body of Christ (1 Cor. 12:27). We also receive spiritual gifts which enable us to minister to others in that body (vv. 4-31).

A spiritual gift is not the same as a natural ability or talent, such as a musical ability, an athletic ability, a high IQ, or a mechanical aptitude. These natural gifts are provided by God to enhance our spiritual gifts.

The root word used for spiritual gift is the noun form of the word grace:

Chara=Joy
Charis=Grace
Charisma=Gift

Joy—grace—gift. Isn't that an attractive concept? Spiritual gifts are also different from the fruit of the Spirit. "But the fruit of the Spirit is love, joy, peace, patience, kindness, goodness, faithfulness, gentleness, self-control; against such things there is no law" (Gal. 5:22-23). God desires these qualities to be evident in every Christian's life.

It is unfortunate that while many believers manifest the fruit of the Spirit, they never discover their own spiritual gift or gifts. Many believers' gifts lie dormant. Because of this, the body of Christ doesn't function as effectively as it could.

Discovering Spiritual Gifts

First, believers should pray to discover their spiritual gifts. Secondly, Christians should become familiar with the variety of gifts which are listed in the Scriptures. Ephesians 4, Romans 12, and 1 Corinthians 12—14 are the primary passages which should be read and studied.

Thirdly, believers should ask themselves the following questions:

1. *What gets spiritual results in my relationship with others?* How does God seem to use me as a blessing? What do I do spiritually that means the most to others?

2. *What do people ask me to do within the body?* The body of Christ often calls out a believer's gifts by asking that person to assume certain responsibilities. Leaders are called on to lead, teachers to teach, givers to give, servers to serve, counselors to counsel.

3. What brings me the most joy in Christ? Doing what you are made to do will result in joy. God has made us so that we really enjoy doing what He wants us to do when it's our higher desire. "For it is God who is at work in you, both to will and to work for His good pleasure" (Phil. 2:13).

4. What irritates me in others? Oftentimes a believer will show a lack of sensitivity in a certain area that I am very concerned about. Usually it is an area that I am particularly aware of because it touches or involves my spiritual strength. In other instances believers seem pushy to me in an area where they have a greater awareness of certain needs. Their response involves trying to meet the need of that area or trying to do something about it because that is their spiritual gift.

For instance, one who has the gift of serving has the motivation to show love by meeting practical needs even before I am aware of the need myself. I mentioned I had a headache one time in the presence of a server. Before I even thought of doing something about it, that person was offering me an aspirin.

When these different perspectives of life collide, they have a tendency to create irritations. Our response, however, should not be to become irritated. Instead, we should recognize our own gifts and likewise the other person's. This will cause us to see the other person's perspective and appreciate his gift, our own, and the God who gave the gifts to us.

These four questions presuppose that a person isn't just a novice in Christ, but is someone with enough maturity to have tried several different areas of service. It would be awfully hard for a teacher to discover he was a teacher if he had not tried to teach. Every believer needs to make an effort in several areas of ministry to see how God uses him the most. We should try to discern in what instances God uses us to build up other believers. How do we know if people are being built up?

When trying to discern our spiritual gift, we should first

find which area of ministry interests us most. If there are two or three areas of interest, we should try all of them. Then we should counsel with those in our fellowship group and get their input. Gifts cannot be discovered in a vacuum. Gifts are given to be used. It is as we use our gifts that they are developed and become more effective for God's glory and for building up of the body of Christ.

It's not really as important that we know the name of our gift as it is that we exercise what God has given us. This means that we fulfill our responsibility to the body of Christ to do the work of the ministry (Eph. 4:12).

For example, one man I know was a highly disciplined, very orderly, effective administrator. It was evident in his personal life, his family life, his walk with God, and his work. It was also evident in his working in the body of Christ. Whether he was asked by his fellowship group or his local church, anytime he was given responsibility for a project, it came off successfully. His involvement gave strength and direction to the project and his discipline and drive always saw it through to the end. The results each time built up the body of Christ. What were his comments on these results? He would say, "That's just God's grace at work. All the glory should go to Him." And indeed, with those words, it did!

This man knew he had the ability to perform such duties because God blessed his efforts. He was not aware that this was the manifestation of a spiritual gift as named in the New Testament. Without knowing this though, he still exercised what God had given him.

Richard Halverson again expresses this principle well:

Be what you are! Simple. . . . But the fact is—many of us find it difficult to accept this fundamental. We keep trying to be what we are not . . . were never intended to be. Life is a constant battle against built-in limitations.

Like trying to be a concert artist when one cannot sing. Instead of accepting ourselves as we are . . . as God made us to be . . . we struggle to be like somebody else. Somebody with different talents and gifts . . . somebody God intended to be unique . . . as He intended each of us to be unique. Intimidated by the seeming superiority of another we ignore our uniqueness. Meanwhile we sacrifice what we are! One will never become what he can be . . . until he accepts what he is! That's reality! You are the only you God gave to the world. . . . Be yourself! Don't deprive the world of you (*Perspective,* Concern Ministries, Inc., January 5, 1977).

The Apostle Paul knew the secret. "I am the least of the apostles, who am not fit to be called an apostle, because I persecuted the church of God. But by the grace of God I am what I am. . . ." (1 Cor. 15:9-10)

What better place to see our gifts develop than in the context of our own fellowship support group? There we may be encouraged to use and develop our gifts in serving one another. Not only that, but the counsel, encouragement, and growth evident in a fellowship support group can launch us on to Christian maturity.

Remember, we need help in *discovering* and developing our spiritual gifts. They can't be discovered alone, nor can they be developed without insight or encouragement from others. "Iron sharpens iron, so one man sharpens another" (Prov. 27:17). "For lack of guidance a nation falls, but many advisers make victory sure" (11:14, NIV).

A Familiar Excuse

A word of caution is appropriate here, however. Some Christians have used their lack of understanding of their spiritual gifts as an excuse not to exercise their God-given responsibilities. For instance, one couple said that they could not help with a Sunday School class of high schoolers because they did not have the gift of teaching. They weren't sure exactly which gifts they *did* have. But until they were certain, they could not be involved in *any* church activities.

When this couple was asked to lead a young couples' class, they again refused on the same grounds. They wanted to know what their gifts were. But they refused to take on any responsibility that might help them discover their gifts!

Christ is the Head of the body. As we are available to Him, He will take care of the *distribution* of gifts. Often the identification of what has been distributed occurs through other people. For example, the pastor and staff of a local congregation should continually strive to aid church members in recognizing their individual gifts.

Likewise, in any fellowship support group the members must continually encourage one another to discover and use their gifts. Often an individual will have a vision for something that needs to be done. The group should tune in to the one expressing such an interest; it could be that person's spiritual gift beckoning him to action. The other group members should encourage that person to help meet that need. When that person uses his spiritual gift to meet such a need, the results can be supernatural.

Spiritual Gifts in Action

Several years ago George Fooshee, who is in the credit collection business, was very concerned about the mounting debts that hinder some Christians from serving the Lord. As our fellowship group discussed his vision and burden, we encouraged him to do something about the problem—perhaps develop some messages on the subject. He not only developed messages but also seminars, and subsequently wrote extensively on the subject.

A pastor in California likewise saw his church explode on this principle. When someone expressed a need that they thought the church should meet, he would ask, "Do you know somebody else who feels this way?" or "Can you find somebody else who feels this way?" His next question was usually, "Why don't the two of you pray about it and see what happens?" This procedure launched many people into the exercise of their own spiritual gifts and into extensive ministries within and from that local church.

People influence each other. When a group freely helps people discover, develop, and distribute their spiritual gifts, the atmosphere is contagious. Through group support, each member is strengthened and encouraged to accomplish what had previously been impossible. Being part of a motivated group can really excite a person. This principle works in business, in voluntary associations, and more so in fellowship support groups—which in addition to the horizontal dynamics, have the very presence of Christ.

Whether we should focus on people's weaknesses or strengths is answered well by the provocative parable of the animal school:

The animals had a school. The curriculum consisted of running, climbing, flying, and swimming. All the animals took all the subjects.

The duck was good in swimming and fair in flying. But he was terrible in running, so he was made to drop his swimming class and stay after school in order to practice his running. He kept this up until he was only average in swimming. But average was acceptable. The others (including the teacher) were no longer threatened by the duck's swimming ability. So everyone felt more comfortable—except the duck.

The eagle was considered a problem student. For instance, in climbing class he beat all others to the top of the tree, but used his own method of getting there. He had to be severely disciplined. Finally, because of non-cooperation in swimming, he was expelled for insubordination.

The rabbit started at the top of the class in running, but was obviously inadequate in other areas. Because of so much make-up work in swimming, he had a nervous breakdown and had to drop out of school.

Of course, the turtle was a failure in most every course offered. His shell was considered to be the leading cause of his failures so it was removed. That did help his running a bit, but sadly he became the first casualty when he was stepped on by a horse.

The faculty was quite disappointed. But all in all it was a good school in humility; there were no real successes. None seemed to measure up to the others. But they did concentrate on their weak points and some progress was made.

Romans 12:3-6 (RSV) says—"For by the grace given to me I bid every one among you not to think of himself more highly than he ought to think, but to think with sober judgment, each according to the measure of faith which God has assigned him. For as in one body we have many members, and all the members do not have the same function, so we, though many, are one body in Christ, and individually members one of another. Having gifts that differ according to the grace given to us, let us use them."

Summing Up

Understanding and being aware of the many varied spiritual gifts stimulates fellowship. We are all different. Too often, we allow our differences to irritate us. When we recognize that many of our differences result from God-given spiritual gifts, accepting one another becomes easier.

In the Book of Ephesians, Paul challenges believers to make every effort to keep the unity of the spirit through the bond of peace (Eph. 4:3). Peter also wrote that we should use our gifts to serve others and faithfully administer God's grace (1 Peter 4:10, NIV). Isn't this a beautiful thought? When we exercise our special gift, we are distributing God's grace to others.

Together let's be informed about our own spiritual gifts, as well as those of others. Let's encourage those in our fellowship group to spiritual growth, to the recognition and development of the spiritual gifts God has given each of us.

Responsible believers are a premium in the body of Christ. Helping develop such believers should be an outgrowth of a fellowship support group.

EIGHT

He's Too Good to Keep

"Gold, gold, gold!" That cry echoed across our land and caused the great California Gold Rush in 1849. Somewhere a miner saw the glitter of gold washed clean by water and the news was too good to keep. He let the word out and it spread like a prairie fire.

In our fellowship groups, we need to recapture the excitement of discovery that Jesus is more valuable than precious metals. "Knowing that you were not redeemed with perishable things like silver or gold from your futile way of life inherited from your forefathers, but with precious blood, as of a lamb unblemished and spotless, the blood of Christ" (1 Peter 1:18-19). Believers in Christ have been washed sparkling clean in God's sight. This is good news and it's easier to share it together.

In fact, our togetherness in Christ is God's weather vane for other people to get to know Him. By our unconditional love and acceptance of one another, we can show unbelievers a way of life that they know nothing about. Jesus prayed that believers would be one so "That the world may

believe" (John 17:21). Once we discover our oneness—
our togetherness—then we need to raise the window shade
and let the world see Him.

Why Should We Share?

"For Christ's love compels us . . . " (2 Cor. 5:14, NIV).
Jesus says that those who love Him keep His commandments
(John 14:21). God has *commanded* our involvement. As
the Father sent Jesus into the world, so Jesus sends us (John
17:18). Jesus came to seek and to save the lost and to give
His life a ransom for many (Luke 19:10; Mark 10:45).

Jesus gave the Great Commission to His disciples, "Go
therefore and make disciples . . . " (Matt. 28:19). The
ascended Lord then told them to wait until they were im-
bued with God's power to fulfill the command to go. When
the Holy Spirit came, He enabled them to be His witnesses,
both in their immediate area, in the surrounding territory,
and to the uttermost part of the world. Believers are God's
active, life-changing agents—no matter where we are. We
are His salt, His light, and His leaven.

Dr. Elton Trueblood once said that these three metaphors
have a common denominator—they are all expendable. Salt
penetrates and preserves only when it gets out of the shaker.
Light expels darkness by expending itself. Eventually, a light
bulb will burn out. We are not to hide our lights under baskets,
but to let them shine.

The third metaphor is that of the leaven. Leaven is mixed
into dough until it permeates the whole. The leaven or yeast
then divides and multiplies itself, thereby losing its individu-
ality. But it makes the dough rise. So also we must be willing
to be expendable for Christ.

As we witness effectively, we'll suffer. Suffering can come
in the form of subtle rejection, open ridicule, or even persecution. But too often we choose not to witness. We're

scared to death. We're afraid—not that people will reject *Christ*—but that they'll reject *us*.

What is our purpose? To be willing servants of others. Do we always expect our pastors to serve us? Too often we feel that pastors are being paid for that purpose. We think they should always be ready to meet our needs. But actually their primary calling is to equip us to minister (Eph. 4:12-13).

How Should We Share?

We should share in humble, yet bold dependence on God. The infinite God delights in people who are so open to Him that they can present His message in a spontaneous way.

Basically there are two ways to share: *verbally* and *nonverbally*. Some modern communication specialists say that nonverbal signals make up over 70 percent of our communicating. This is why John said, "Let us not love with word or with tongue, but in deed and truth" (1 John 3:18). Our spoken messages are proven (or disproven) by our silent actions. We should ask ourselves: *Do I have genuine concern for others?* When we become more concerned for our friends than for their opinions of us, then we're motivated to share the Gospel.

Do we really believe there are only two alternatives after death? Jesus did. Twenty-two times in the New Testament, *hell* is mentioned—sixteen of those were by Jesus Himself. He was so concerned about our eternal destiny that He died on the cross.

It's not easy to keep a spiritual perspective when we're surrounded by worldliness. God wants the best for others. We need to love others in such a way that they can understand God's offer of love and make their own choices.

As J.I. Packer puts it in *Evangelism and the Sovereignty of God*, "Our calling as Christians is not to love God's elect, and them only, but to love our neighbor, irrespective of whether he is elect or not. Now, the nature of love is to do good and to relieve need. If, then, our neighbor is unconverted, we are to show love to him as best we can by seeking to share with him the Good News without which he must needs perish. So we find Paul warning and teaching 'every man'; not merely because he was an apostle, but because every man was his neighbor. And the measure of the urgency of our evangelistic task is the greatness of our neighbor's need and the immediacy of his danger" (InterVarsity Press, pp. 99-100).

Nonverbal Communication

The principles in God's Word teach integrity and humility. "Make it your ambition to lead a quiet life, to mind your own business and to work with your hands, just as we told you, so that your daily life may win the respect of outsiders and so that you will not be dependent on anybody" (1 Thes. 4:11-12, NIV). We are called to walk worthy of our vocation. Let's develop an expertise in our business, whatever it is—to do it heartily for God's glory.

One of the outstanding examples of nonverbal communication is Mother Teresa, that remarkable nun headquartered in Calcutta, India. She received the 1979 Nobel Peace Prize for her work among the poor. In Calcutta she ministers to the needs of the "poorest of the poor" in that area and through her order, the "Missionaries of Charity," to the poor in other cities of the world. One of her prayers describes her group's orientation, "Make us worthy, Lord, to serve our fellowmen throughout the world who live and die in poverty and hunger. Give them through our hands this day their daily bread, and by our understanding love, give peace and joy." Mother Teresa has been quoted by Malcolm Muggeridge as saying, "Love is a fruit in season at all times" (*Something Beautiful for God,* Ballantine Books, p. 47).

I would to God that we could all take Mother Teresa's humble attitude in our work. She says, "Let there be no pride or vanity in the work. The work is God's work, the poor are God's poor. Put yourself completely under the influence of Jesus, so that He may think His thoughts in your mind, do His work through your hands, for you will be all-powerful with Him who strengthens you" (*Something Beautiful*, p. 49).

On the other side of the coin, Paul asks, "How then shall they call upon Him in whom they have not believed? And how shall they believe in Him whom they have not heard? And how shall they hear without a preacher?" (Rom. 10:14) Indeed, how *will* others hear unless we tell them?

Verbal Communication

It is through preaching that God saves people. People need to hear God's message. Watching Christians live godly lives won't save unbelievers.

Some years ago at a Billy Graham Crusade in the Northwest a businessman heard God's message. He went forward during the Crusade and trusted Christ for his salvation. He was so excited that he went back to tell his longtime associate, who patiently listened to his story. His partner expressed his delight. He thought the man's decision was wonderful. To this response the new believer asked, "What do you mean wonderful? Do you really know what I am talking about?"

"Oh, yes," his partner replied, "I've been a believer in Christ for many, many years. In fact, I teach Sunday School down at our church."

The businessman was dismayed. "You mean to tell me that all these years you have known this about Christ and never shared it with me? I've watched your life and admired it. I've observed your honesty and tried to emulate it. I've coveted your morality and tried to duplicate it. But you *never* told me how to find the Source."

Let's not stop short in our communication. Together we can have a nonverbal witness by being models of Christ's love with one another, with our families, with our associates, or anyone with whom we come in contact. But, let's also encourage one another to discover creative ways to talk about the Source of life. As we take time in a group meeting to report on our witnessing activities, we can spur one another on to greater productivity for God.

In a personal letter to me, Charles Colson pointed out, "The small group should be a launching pad to send people into the world to live their faith, never an escape. The great danger here is that people find personal fulfillment in the prayer meeting and they think that's the purpose of it. It isn't, though everything in our culture makes us think that self-gratification is the goal of life. The small group is to equip you to live as a Christian 24 hours a day."

There are a lot of good methods to use that can help an interested person establish his relationship with Christ. Each believer should find a method that works for him and use it. This suggestion is similar to Dwight L. Moody's position. When he was challenged that his soul-winning method was poor, he replied something like this: "Well, I don't like it much either. What's your method?" To which his critic responded, "I have no method." Mr. Moody answered, "Then I believe I like my poor method better than your no method."

Hindrances to Communicating

The devil, the world, and we ourselves set up obstacles to witnessing. The weapons of our guerrilla warfare, however, are intangible. We have the spiritual equipment of Ephesians 6—and the mightiest weapon of all, prayer. Unless people become spiritually quickened by God's Spirit, they cannot break out of the enemies' camp. But as we pray individually and together, we overcome the devil and the world.

We need also to pray for ourselves. In the first recorded prayer meeting in the Book of Acts, the believers prayed for boldness in witnessing. In Acts 4, Peter and John reported to the other believers about the threats made by the Jewish religious leaders. Peter and John had been told not to speak of or teach in the name of Jesus (vv. 18, 21, 23). The group responded with prayer. They even prayed for themselves. "Consider their threats and enable Your servants to speak Your word with great boldness. After they prayed, the place where they were meeting was shaken. And they were all filled with the Holy Spirit and spoke the Word of God boldly" (Acts 4:29, 31, NIV). For many of us, this same prayer for boldness is what we need the most to overcome hindrances.

The Lifestyle of Verbal Communication

Jesus, in Matthew 13:3-9, gave us the "Parable of the Sower," to explain to us the lifestyle of verbal witnessing. Later, He told the meaning of the parable:

Listen then to what the parable of the sower means. When anyone hears the message about the kingdom and does not understand it, the evil one comes and snatches away what was sown in his heart. This is the seed sown along the path. What was sown on rocky places is the man who hears the word and at once receives it with joy. But since he has no root, he lasts only a short time. When trouble or persecution comes because of the word, he quickly falls away. What was sown among the thorns is the man who hears the word, but the worries of this life and the deceitfulness of wealth choke it, making it unfruitful. But what was sown on good soil is the man who hears the word and understands it. He produces a crop, yielding a hundred, sixty or thirty times what was sown (vv. 18-23, NIV).

Let's be faithful and ready to sow the good seed—productive in our Lord's service.

As my friend, Dr. Leighton Ford says, "Don't keep the faith—give it away." By following the scriptural pattern, we can do this not only in our immediate and surrounding areas, but in *all the world*.

NINE

A Fresh Vision for Small Group Prayer

It is exciting to look out and see a beautiful, God-created world and its most exciting attraction—the men and women who inhabit it! But so often we see only the grit, the grime, the irritations, and the problems. Indeed, we live in a problem-oriented society; even the church has become problem-oriented. So what's the problem? The fact is that not enough of us have Christ's vision!

Do we look at people with Christ's eyes? Do we love them as *He* wants us to? Christ sees the potential in every individual to become like Him—to become conformed to His image. Yet, He also sees the individual's present need. That's one reason He became our Saviour—in order to meet our needs.

Adjusting Our Spiritual Bifocals

But how can we maintain His vision? How can we look at the world optimistically, yet realistically? Individually and together we must wear spiritual bifocals to see God's vision. Only then can we recognize the spiritual meanings of life.

Bifocals have two lenses. The small lens of our spiritual bifocals help us see our immediate relationships and the tasks at hand, to see where we are. The big lens helps us look at the whole world. Through that big lens we see the needs of the community at large, our state, our nation, and our world.

Paul urged Timothy:

First of all, that requests, prayers, intercession and thanksgiving be made for everyone—for kings and all those in authority, that we may live peaceful and quiet lives in all godliness and holiness. This is good, and pleases God our Saviour, who wants all men to be saved and to come to a knowledge of the truth. For there is one God and one Mediator between God and men, the man Christ Jesus, who gave Himself as a ransom for all men (1 Tim. 2:1-6, NIV).

Other than evangelistic efforts, the major dynamic that can keep a fellowship group from becoming ingrown and self-centered is prayer for the world. We must remember that "God so loved the world" (John 3:16) and this condition continually remains true. We need to allow God to express His love through our prayers, our availability, and our involvement.

There is a great mystery in prayer, but "The prayer of a righteous man is powerful and effective" (James 5:16b, NIV). Do we really believe this? Are we praying for people as they are brought to our attention through the news media or some other form of communication? As we are alerted to world situations, do we prayerfully bring these before the Lord? Through prayer the large lens on our spiritual bifocals stays clean and strengthens our sight. The principle is simple: Prayer keeps our vision clear and our lenses clean.

Let's look at Abraham's encounter with God in Genesis 18. "And the Lord said, 'The outcry of Sodom and Gomorrah is indeed great, and their sin is exceedingly grave'" (v. 20). Then Abraham approached Him and said: "Suppose there are fifty righteous within the city; wilt Thou indeed sweep it away and not spare the place for the sake of the fifty righteous who are in it?" (v. 24) The Lord answered Abraham's query, "If I find in Sodom fifty righteous within the city, then I will spare the whole place on their account" (v. 26).

This conversation between Abraham and the Lord continued, reducing more and more the number of righteous people that could be saved in the wicked cities of Sodom and Gomorrah. Finally Abraham asked, "Oh may the Lord not be angry, and I shall speak only this once; suppose ten are found there?" And He said, "I will not destroy it on account of the ten" (v. 32).

Amazingly, the Lord was willing to spare the two most wicked cities in history for the sake of 10 righteous people. Unfortunately, He did not find any such people. Scripture records the cities' destruction. Perhaps, if a few citizens had been praying, Sodom and Gomorrah would not have been destroyed.

The Importance of Praise

An important part of prayer is to thank God for what we see Him doing. For example, we have tremendous opportunities to give thanks and praise to the Lord for the good reports we hear from other places. "Like cold water to a weary soul, so is good news from a distant land" (Prov. 25:25).

Spiritual bifocals help us discern what God has done and is doing so that we might praise and thank Him. Whether it be news of a famous athlete confessing his faith in Christ on television, or the report of an obscure peasant behind the Iron Curtain trusting in the Lord, we can praise God.

The athlete on TV witnesses to millions. The peasant's conversion also thrills us—for one individual in God's economy is of infinite worth.

God works in as many varied ways as there are people on this earth. We should recognize His individual care and indescribable love for us and praise Him for it. But, more than that, we should share His care, His love, and His compassion.

Jesus' Last Words

Dr. Howard Hendricks, the outstanding Christian communicator, asks, "If your closest friend is dying and you're at his bedside leaning over to hear his last words, will you remember what he said?" (Layman's HELP Seminar, 1977) The Lord Jesus Christ in His last words commanded, "Go therefore and make disciples of all the nations, baptizing them in the name of the Father and the Son and the Holy Spirit, teaching them to observe all that I commanded you; and lo, I am with you always, even to the end of the age" (Matt. 28:19-20).

It is not the length of this commandment that makes it the Great Commission. Rather, because of its strategic timing and source, it has become our motivation for sharing our faith. One of Christ's reactions to looking out on His world is recorded by Matthew: "And seeing the multitudes, He felt compassion for them, because they were distressed and downcast like sheep without a shepherd. Then He said to His disciples, 'The harvest is plentiful, but the workers are few. Therefore beseech the Lord of the harvest to send out workers into His harvest' " (Matt. 9:36-38).

What is our reaction? Do we look? Is compassion our feeling? Do we see the white fields? Is prayer to the Father our response? Is our lens clean?

Too often we cannot see God's world vision. His purposes

go unseen because believers find themselves either in a deep rut of local self-interest or looking only through their natural eyes. These are the eyes of the pleasure-seeker—with only a horizontal perspective.

Jesus' concern was primarily spiritual and global. Although He personally traveled less in His lifetime than many of us do in one day (never going more than 200 miles from where He was born), He said we were to go into *all* the world.

Spiritual Multiplication

Today there are about 4½ billion people on earth. If each of the approximate 1 billion who name the name of Christ (all the Protestants, Roman Catholics, and Greek Orthodox who believe in the virgin birth, sacrificial death, and resurrection of Jesus Christ) would win one person a year and train that one to repeat the process, we could mathematically reach the whole world for Christ in less than three years! If only 10 percent of those professing Christianity would be faithfully winning and training one a year, it would take just five and one half years.

Of course, there are some countries and cultures that desperately need missionaries and witnesses from outside in order to plant this leavening influence, but leaven or yeast increases by multiplication. Jesus said, "The kingdom of heaven is like yeast that a woman took and mixed into a large amount of flour until it worked all through the dough" (Matt. 13:33, NIV).

The principle of multiplication is the great dynamic that makes pioneer missionary efforts meaningful to other countries and cultures. Sometimes these efforts appear to result in relatively few believers. However, every convert has the potential to reach many others. "The least of you will become a thousand, the smallest a mighty nation. I am the Lord; in its time I will do this swiftly" (Isa. 60:22, NIV).

Some of the reasons why this multiplication principle is so important were set forth by the 19th-century missionary, Roland Allen. Writing at about the turn of this century in *The Spontaneous Expansion of the Church*, he said:

> Our missionaries must aim at laying such a foundation that India may be evangelized by Indians, China by Chinese, Africa by Africans, each country by its own Christians. That certainly must mean that our missions ought to prepare the way for the evangelization of the country by the free spontaneous activity of our converts, and that their success must be measured not so much by the number of foreign missionaries employed, or by the number of converts, as by the growth of a native church in the power to expand.
>
> The great things of God are beyond our control. Therein lies a vast hope. Spontaneous expansion could fill the continents with the knowledge of Christ: our control cannot reach as far as that. We constantly bewail our limitations: open doors unentered; doors closed to us as foreign missionaries; fields white to the harvest which we cannot reap. Spontaneous expansion could enter open doors, force closed ones; and reap those white fields. Our control cannot: it can only appeal pitifully for more men to maintain control. . . .
>
> We are quite ready to talk of self-supporting, self-extending, and self-governing churches in the abstract as ideals; but the moment that we think of ourselves as establishing self-supporting, self-governing churches in the biblical sense we are met by this fear, a terrible, deadly fear. Suppose they really were self-supporting, and depended no longer on our support, where should we be? Suppose self-extension were really self-extension, and we could not control it, what would happen? Sup-

pose they were really self-governing, how would they govern? We instinctively think of something which we cannot control as tending to disorder (Eerdmans, pp. 13, 19).

None of us can go to every part of the world but together we can have world-wide influence through effectual prayer. If all of us are available to our God, to love and serve Him wherever He sends us, we'll complete this task which He has given. Let's not let the world, the flesh, or the devil rob us of our faith, hope, and vision for world-wide evangelization.

Sometimes we find ourselves lacking because of a clouded viewpoint, one fogged over by our own limited perspectives. The blinders of our own activities limit our vision of what God might do. In an age where our communication abilities are at a peak, we lack the vision to see God move. We have a dirty lens and, through prayer, we must ask God to wipe it clean.

The Laymen's Prayer Revival

For a fresh vision of what might happen, should believers decide to let their fellowship really launch their belief and faith in what God can do, let's consider what He has done. Let's take a look at some aspects of the great Laymen's Prayer Revival of 1858. J. Edwin Orr, one of the foremost scholars of American revivalism, explains briefly why you may have never heard of this great revival: "The shelves of the university and seminary libraries in the United States are generally well-stocked with volumes dealing with the revivals of religion led by Jonathan Edwards, George Whitefield, Charles Finney, Dwight Moody, and other men of lesser fame. In striking contrast, the great religious awakening of 1858 has been sadly neglected despite the fact that it has outshone its predecessors in intensity and lasting results" (*The Fervent Prayer*, Moody Press, p. 5).

This revival came at a time of political strife and social unrest. Financially there had been a boom. Gold was discovered in '49 in the West. Trade and immigration were flourishing, but in 1858 there was an economic collapse. Interest rates jumped to as high as 60 percent per year (and we think *we* have high interest rates!). Banks and businesses closed. At one time there were 30,000 men in New York City out of work.

Out of this background came a layman by the name of Jeremiah Lanphier, a zealous 40-year-old businessman. He became involved in inner-city missionary work in New York City. Recalling his inspiration to the task he said, "Going my rounds in the performance of my duties one day, as I was walking along the streets, the idea was suggested to my mind that an hour of prayer, from 12 to 1 o'clock, would be beneficial to businessmen."

However, Lanphier was not the Dwight L. Moody or Billy Graham of his day. Dr. Orr has suggested that another reason this significant movement may have been ignored is that "no great leader produced the revival, and the revival did not immediately produce any great figure" (*The Fervent Prayer*, p. 6).

Dr. John Hannah, professor of historical theology at Dallas Theological Seminary, gives insight into the beginning of the movement. (The opening quote is from historian Russell Francis.)

"From his (Lanphier's) contact and consultation with Colgate's committee, there evolved the idea of the joint-sponsorship of a meeting that would be shared by members of all evangelical churches." The first such meeting was announced for September 23, 1857 in the third floor of the "Consistory" of the Old Dutch Reformed Church on Fulton Street and 6 people were in attendance. . . . On September 30, 20 met for prayer and when 40 came on October 7 the meetings became daily. By mid-January the Consistory was filled on all three floors and many were turned away; attendance reached 3,000.

As a result other locations were sought to hold the meetings throughout the city until "by spring more than a score of such meetings were in operation." In February the John Street Methodist Church started meetings under YMCA auspices, and in March, Burton's Theatre was used, which was located near city hall. . . . At the peak of interest, some 21 daily meetings were held in Manhattan with 6 others in Brooklyn. Meetings were held at various times throughout the day to accommodate the businessman with locations and places announced daily ("The Laymen's Prayer Revival of 1858," *Bibliotheca Sacra,* January-March 1977, pp. 64-65).

Results of the Revival

As the historical account indicates, the revival began as a single prayer meeting. Then it spread to Philadelphia, Albany, Boston, Buffalo, Pittsburgh, Cleveland, Cincinnati, Detroit, Indianapolis, Chicago, St. Louis, Omaha, and even to the Pacific Coast! It was indeed a revival of spontaneous growth.

The number of converts during the revival best illustrates what happens when saints gather together and pray, really believing God. In a look at the history of revivalism, Frank G. Beardsley has estimated this phenomenal movement of the Spirit of God across our land in terms of the number of professions of faith: "During several weeks when the revival was at high tide it was estimated that 50,000 people were converted to God. . . . Total number of conversions ran as high as 1 million" (*Religious Progress Through Religious Re-*

vivals, American Tract Society, p. 47). The significance of those numbers is gripping when we realize that the total U.S. population at that time was only 30 million.

But the revival did not stop there. Dr. Hannah notes, "The revival began prior to the great civil holocaust of 1861-1865, but continued unabated through the war and to the turn of the century. Estimates of conversions are listed between 300,000 and 1 million, over 100,000 alone in the Confederate Army" ("The Laymen's Prayer Revival," p. 59).

The results continued in many ways. Campus revivals swept the country. Youth were spurred to serve the Lord in ways unprecedented in our country's history. Literally dozens of significant lay ministries sprang up all over. The Salvation Army was formed in America and its ministry of evangelism and social uplift has continued to today. The YMCA was successfully transplanted to America from England, resulting in the conversions of thousands of young men and women.

Probably the most evident result of the revival remaining in our country today is the Sunday School. The Laymen's Prayer Revival had a direct hand in the emergence of the Sunday School movement in the latter half of the 19th century. Another movement still remaining from this revival is the Keswick Convention. It came out of the holiness movement touched off by the impact of the prayer revival in Methodist circles.

Have you ever sung, "Stand Up, Stand Up for Jesus" by George Duffield? Or, how about "Almost Persuaded" by P.P. Bliss? Both these people, along with others such as Ira Sankey and Elizabeth Cecilia Clephane, were stirred by the revival to write many of the great hymns which we still sing today.

Indeed, the Laymen's Prayer Revival of 1858 impacted the world for Jesus Christ. Why? Because God chose to move. But, also, men dared to believe God! They met together in biblical fellowship. They believed God for what He can do.

They prayed. For world vision, nothing is more inspiring than to realize the impetus provided by the prayers of the revival. Their influence was staggering.

Worldwide Results of the Revival

Laymen and college youth alike responded to God's call to overseas ministries. Men like D. L. Moody were motivated by the Lord as laymen to preach the Word of God to a world desperately in need of His truth. As Moody preached throughout America and England in the 1880's college students began to respond to the call to missions and emerged into an international student movement. The "Cambridge Seven" was formed and cricket star C.T. Studd turned his life from athletics to the service of God on the mission field. From there the Student Volunteer Movement developed in 1886.

The Holy Spirit opened the eyes of those praying for the need of the world for the God of the Bible. Dr. Orr has said that the great story of the Holy Spirit's movement in the student awakenings of this era cannot be divorced from the course of missions in countries overseas. The following is a paraphrased digest from Orr's *Campus Aflame*, summarizing the effects of the prayers of the revival and the resulting student involvement in missions:

Africa
The 1858-59 Awakenings in the United States and the United Kingdom were followed by similar movements in South Africa, beginning among the Zulus . . . through the visit of William Taylor of California . . . using Southern Africa as a base, missionary societies penetrated Central Africa. . . .

India
The 1858-59 Awakenings were felt in India in the 1860s. Not only did they bring out a contingent of dedi-

cated missionaries, but they stirred the Indian Christian communities too. . . . Within 30 years of 1860, there were 2,418 institutions of all classes and grades with 104,616 pupils. . . .

China

During the 1859 Awakening in Wales, David Morgan conducted a meeting in a Carmarthen village, reporting pessimistically, "It was a very hard service." One of the converts, a lad named Timothy Richard, went to China and became the best-known and most influential Baptist worker. . . .

Japan

One of the first pioneer missionaries to Japan, J.C. Hepburn, a Presbyterian, arrived in 1859. . . . Within 30 years of the opening of Japan, Protestant missionaries had established 250 churches . . . with 25,000 members, and they operated 100 schools with 10,000 pupils.

South America

Immigration had opened the closed doors of the southern Latin American countries. Americans from the Army of the Confederacy found a promising colony in Brazil, and found a missionary permanently settled there since 1859.

Ireland-Scotland-England

News of the American Awakening amazed the Christians in the United Kingdom, but not long afterward the same sort of movement manifested itself in the North of Ireland. . . . In 1859, however, the Revival in Ulster resembled the frontier awakenings in producing such intense conviction of sin that physical prostration occurred in 10 percent of the converts. The social impact was as astounding as it was lasting. . . . The same awakening followed in Scotland, with similar results. . . . At the same time as the Irish Revival, a movement began in Wales, with a wholesome transformation of society. . . . In England, the awakening began in 1860 and spread to every county, reaching every class and condition. . . . (Moody Press, pp. 71, 75-78, 68)

Africa, India, China, the world! God has demonstrated in history what happens when He chooses to move. Abraham, Moses, the prophets, Paul, James, Saint Augustine, Martin Luther, John Calvin, the Reformation, the First Great Awakening, the Laymen's Prayer Revival . . . all are demonstrations of God's grace. They are demonstrations that God wants men to gather in His name, to offer praise and thanksgiving for what He has done, to offer supplication that He might do more.

Revive Us Again

How then should we proceed? Above all we must remember that revival is entirely dependent on the sovereignty of God. We must not think of revival as a combination lock which opens when we turn it correctly. God often responds in ways we might never expect! How should believers pray who really desire to see God move in a significant way as He has done in the past?

Let's first begin with our own lives. Take a look at your own priorities and values. Ask God to straighten out your own life first—to help you get yourself in order. Give Christ top priority in your life.

Your family and friends are next. Are they following Christ? Are they adequately representing Him? What are their needs? Are you serving them?

Finally, prayer together should aim at other believers as a

high priority. We are to be concerned with all men in prayer, especially those of the household of faith. They are spiritual kinsmen and we are responsible to bear one another's burdens and support one another through prayer. We are engaged in a spiritual warfare and one of the mightiest weapons we have in our arsenal is prayer. Too often, however, instead of being utilized by squads of the Master's army, that is just where we find this weapon located . . . in the arsenel gathering dust. When Paul describes the armor for our spiritual warfare, he gives us a long list of equipment:

> Finally, be strong in the Lord, and in the strength of His might. Put on the full armor of God, that you may be able to stand firm against the schemes of the devil. For our struggle is not against flesh and blood, but against the rulers, against the powers, against the world forces of this darkness, against the spiritual forces of wickedness in the heavenly places. Therefore, take up the full armor of God, that you may be able to resist in the evil day, and having done everything, to stand firm. Stand firm therefore, having girded your loins with truth, and having put on the breastplate of righteousness, and having shod your feet with the preparation of the Gospel of peace; in addition to all, taking up the shield of faith with which you will be able to extinguish all the flaming missiles of the evil one. And take the helmet of salvation, and the sword of the Spirit, which is the Word of God (Eph. 6:10-17).

Then, after fully explaining the soldier's equipment, he concludes the passage with the admonishment to pray in the Spirit on *all* occasions with *all* kinds of prayers and requests:

"And pray in the Spirit on all occasions with all kinds of

prayers and requests. With this in mind, be alert and always keep on praying for all the saints" (v. 18, NIV).

The army of Christ is to go forward on its knees! That army has done so before! Valiant soldiers of the Cross have prayed. God has answered. As Jeremiah Lanphier and the lay believers of the great 1858 Prayer Revival fell to their knees, their society was touched. A worldwide impact resulted when God chose to move through those believers who were willing to fellowship together with prayer at the core of their group involvement.

Wouldn't it be wonderful if we could again see God give us such a spontaneous lay movement? Let's pray that God will use all of His people, whether clergy in vocational Christian service or laymen. We have an unprecedented opportunity to respond to our royal call to be His ambassadors to the whole world, beginning right where we are now! Perhaps God will again do what only *He* can do: sweep our world with a spiritual prairie fire!

It is so simple. God wants just two things. He wants us to be His people. And He wants us, His people, to represent Him for His glory! As David exclaimed in Psalm 34:3, "O magnify the Lord with me, and let us exalt His name together."

TEN

Action Steps for Enriching Fellowship

People may be classified in many and various categories. For the purposes of this book, we will view only two classifications: those who *are not* of a small group fellowship; and those who *are* of a small group fellowship. It is our hope that if you are in the former category, this chapter will give you some practical "how-to's" on getting a small group started. Every follower of Christ needs the support of a fellowship group. Together is the way to grow, to know Him, to love Him, and to serve Him.

If You Are Not in a Group

1. *Pray.* Pray for at least one, or several people, whom God would have you relate to in a small group. The best way to get started is by prayer. When God brings people together, prayer works. Often we try to superimpose our desires for fellowship on an existing group such as a Sunday School class, Bible study, or a ladies' circle. Many times the common bond in these groups is something other than a desire for fellowship. Trying to force fellowship on other people is not the best way

to start a group. The best way is to identify others who have a genuine interest which is an inside desire to share in fellowship. The question is how to identify those who are interested. The answer is prayer.

2. *Invite those who are interested* to meet together and discuss the concept. As a general rule, the smaller the group, the sooner your fellowship will deepen. Three or four people are enough. In fact, Jesus promised His presence where two or three are gathered in His name. So if you begin with only one other like-minded person you have His promised presence. Some students of group dynamics indicate it is probably better to keep an odd number in the group—three, five, seven, etc. The principles set forth in this book are not only applicable to small groups but often are important in individual relationships.

3. *Start on a trial basis.* Make a commitment to meet for a limited time. If you are meeting weekly, perhaps you can meet for six weeks. At the end of that period, take time to evaluate the group's effectiveness. Group members should decide if they want to continue their participation. If not, then they can easily end their involvement without embarrassment or pressure. For those who want to continue, you should agree together on ground rules. Some groups even formalize these agreements in the form of a covenant with one another.

Ground Rules

Who should lead? Spiritually, Christ is the Head of the body. Each group should function somewhat like a theocracy. As Jesus said, "But do not be called Rabbi; for One is your Teacher, and you are all brothers. And do not call anyone on earth your father; for One is your Father, He who is in heaven. And do not be called leaders; for One is your Leader, that is, Christ" (Matt. 23:8-10).

Of course Christ many times delegates His leadership

through people and the leadership of a group depends on the group's level of spiritual maturity. Many groups function smoothly without an appointed leader. But members of groups without leaders must be mature enough to recognize Christ's headship and sensitive to His leadership through submission to one another. God can lead very effectively through the gifts of all those participating without a chairman.

When a group is less mature, perhaps has several new converts or some problem-laden individuals, then it is desirable to have a very strong leader whom God can use. Between these two choices, probably somewhere in between, select the variation with which your particular group will be most comfortable. Be careful to avoid participating in a group where powerful personalities try to manipulate weaker ones.

How to lead. Christ gave us an interesting leadership principle recorded in the Book of Mark. "For even the Son of man did not come to be served, but to serve, and to give His life a ransom for many" (Mark 10:45). He put this principle into practice when He washed His disciples' feet (John 13).

A Christian leader should be a servant; a leader who thinks first of others and of their needs. This kind of leader is willing to be personally vulnerable, to speak openly and candidly of his own needs, thereby setting a tone of openness, love, and unconditional acceptance. This kind of leader creates an atmosphere of honest interaction.

What are the mechanics of meeting? This varies with the desires of the participants, but questions any group needs to discuss are:

When? It is recommended that groups meet weekly. Biweekly is as infrequent as any group should meet to keep current on one another's needs.

Where? Meetings can be held in a home, restaurant, office, motel meeting room, corner of a factory, or in

any location which will afford the privacy necessary for at least one hour without interruptions.
Format? Sharing, caring, praying, studying, reporting.

If You Are in a Group

If you're in a group now and would like to stimulate your fellowship, take the following quiz. (Question one corresponds to chapter one, question two corresponds to chapter two, and so on.)

	Yes	No
1. a. Is spiritual zip and excitement missing?		
b. Are we progressively growing together in our knowledge of Christ?		
c. Do we tend to counsel one another and filter life's situations through the framework of the Word of God?		
2. a. Is my group growing in love for one another?		
b. There seem to be barriers between some of our participants.		
c. I sometimes sense rejection from others.		
3. a. Do I ask first how others are doing?		
b. Do some members of my group focus first on their own situations, circumstances, and prayer requests?		
c. Together do we seek Christ's view of things?		

	Yes	No

d. Together do we take the responsibility for helping one another in keeping priorities straight?

e. Are we consistently praying for each other's concerns and reporting on answers?

f. Are we accountable to each other for our progress toward full maturity in Christ?

4. a. Do we all clearly understand God's ultimate goal for us as individuals on this earth?

b. Do we seriously seek to cooperate with God by helping one another take the next step or steps which God desires?

5. a. Oftentimes the group appears disjointed with each one going his own way.

b. Generally we do not voluntarily bring before our group major personal decisions before they're reached.

c. When the participants in my group ask me about personal affairs, I feel they are meddling.

d. I listen to counsel but *I always* reserve the right to make my final decision.

	Yes	No

6. a. We're all aware that the single most important thing we can do together is *believe* God.   ____   ____

   b. We pray together for other believers in our community.   ____   ____

   c. Generally the anxiety level is pretty high among some of our group members.   ____   ____

7. a. I believe every Christian has a spiritual gift.   ____   ____

   b. My group is aware that I've identified at least one spiritual gift God has given me.   ____   ____

   c. We actively seek to help one another discover and develop spiritual gifts.   ____   ____

   d. We actively challenge and encourage one another in the use of respective strengths.   ____   ____

8. a. Together we exhibit a real concern for those who do not yet know Christ.   ____   ____

   b. We encourage each other in seeking and using opportunities to share our faith.   ____   ____

   c. We pray for boldness.   ____   ____

9. a. We discuss and pray for those in other countries.   ____   ____

   b. We pray for our president and others in government.   ____   ____

	Yes	No

c. We consistently pray for
our daily tasks, and those
people in our immediate
sphere of influence.

d. We are asking God for a
worldwide, all-inclusive lay
movement, by which God might
bring many to know and serve
Him.

10. Instead of questions for this chapter, let's consider a few
more aspects of the Laymen's Prayer Revival of 1858.
The following exhibits will give us an overview of the
mechanics of the movement: its programs, meeting format, characteristics, and reactions to its impact as recorded during the very times in which it occurred.

General Characteristics of the Revival of 1858

Remember these facts from the Laymen's Prayer Revival of
1858. They are the characteristics which distinguished the
revival, marking it as a distinct movement of God's Spirit
across our land. Our prayer is that God might cause these
characteristics to pop up again in fellowship groups around the
country. Should He say yes to that prayer, we too might see
the revival fires burn.

• The movement was almost exclusively made up of laymen who cooperated wholeheartedly with the Lord and with
each other.

• Practically all the revival's meetings sprang up spontan-
eously. No organization or denomination planned it or promoted it. A few people just decided to have biblical fellowship
with prayer at the core.

- The revival was nonsectarian, with a sense of godly harmony pervading the movement. No matter what denomination or organization one belonged to, the desire was to cooperate with God and with others.
- There was a lack of emotional excess during the revival. People were not out to get on a temporary "high." They desired to pray and to serve the Lord.
- The meetings focused on prayer, everything else being of lower priority.
- The meetings started in the cities then filtered down to the rural communities, in contrast to earlier revivals.
- The revival was widely publicized by newspapers, which generated great public interest.
- The meetings were particularly characterized by promptness as to time. There were no "extended meetings," no "one more stanza's" of invitation hymns. The meetings were reverent, direct, and to the point. They began at 12 o'clock and ended promptly at 1 P.M.

Program Format for Meetings

Here we include the format of the prayer meetings during the revival. The intention is not to suggest that we go back to this format today, but only to demonstrate the disciplined manner of the meetings. Leaders of the meetings were given a strict schedule by which to conduct the one-hour affairs.

Please Observe the Following Rules:

Be prompt, commencing precisely at 12 o'clock.
The Leader is not expected to exceed 10 minutes in opening the meeting.

1st   Open the meeting by reading and singing from three to five verses of a hymn.
2nd   Prayer
3rd   Read a portion of the Scripture.

4th   Say the meeting is now open for prayers and exhortations, observing particularly the rules overhead, inviting the brethren from abroad to take part in the services.

5th   Read but one or two requests at a time—*requiring* a prayer to follow—such prayer to have special reference to the same.

6th   In case of any suggestion or proposition by any person, say this is simply a prayer meeting, and that they are out of order, and call on some brother to pray.

7th   Give out the closing hymn five minutes before 1 o'clock. Request the benediction from a clergyman, if one be present (From J. Edwin Orr, *The Fervent Prayer,* p. 35).

A placard was hung on the wall, in a prominent place commanding the attention of the whole meeting. It read something like this:

Brethren are earnestly requested to adhere to the five-minute rule. Prayers and exhortations not to exceed five minutes in order to give all an opportunity. Not more than two consecutive prayers or exhortations. No controverted points discussed.

Denominational Figures and Reactions

For those who use the yardstick of church growth as the measure of an effective revival, the following figures clearly demonstrate that the Prayer Revival had a great impact. However, this is not the only, nor necessarily the best, criteria for measuring a revival's effectiveness. (These figures are from J. Edwin Orr, *The Second Evangelical Awakening in America,* Marshall, Morgan and Scott, p. 65):

1. Methodists
   Methodist Episcopal Church   135,527 new members
   Methodist Episcopal Church,
      South   43,338 new members
   Other Methodist bodies reporting   37,165 new members

                  216,030 total

2. Baptists
   American Baptists (North &
      South)   92,243 new members
   Free Will Baptists   5,714 new members
   Other Baptist bodies reporting   8,043 new members

                  106,000 total

3. Presbyterians   34,650 new members

4. Congregationalists   21,582 new members

5. Protestant Episcopal Church   14,822 new members

6. Dutch Reformed   10,065 new members

For 1858 alone . . .

         GRAND TOTAL   403,149 new members!

Denominational Reactions

J. Edwin Orr, in *The Fervent Prayer* (pp. 38, 42), records reactions from some denominational journals of the day. First is a description of the revival by Bishop McIlaine, an Episcopal minister of the era. He notes some characteristics of the revival: "(1) Few sermons had to be preached; (2) lay brethren were eager to witness; (3) seekers flocked to the altar; (4) nearly every seeker had been blessed; (5) experiences enjoyed remained clear; (6) converts were filled with holy boldness; (7) religion became a daytime social topic; (8) family altars were strengthened; (9) testimony given nightly was abundant; and (10) conversation was marked by a pervading seriousness."

A Methodist journal described the revival another way: "(1) Simple in means, prayer, reading, brief exposition, and singing; (2) quiet, marked by calmness and freedom from unwholesome excitement; (3) harmonious, showing brotherly affection; (4) restrained, having a conservative influence; (5) far-reaching, of a very wide extent; and (6) reputable, commanding the respect of the world in unprecedented ways, all of which was easily substantiated" (Orr, *The Fervent Prayer,* p. 42).

An Exhortation to World Prayer

Dr. Billy Graham at the Lausanne International Congress on World Evangelization in 1974, expressed his reaction to the television view of the world as relayed to earth from our astronauts on the moon. He said he thought it looked so small he "wanted to reach out and grab it for Christ." As Isaiah said, "Look unto Me, and be ye saved, all the ends of the earth: for I am God, and there is none else" (Isa. 45:22, KJV).

A world map gives a good view of what Dr. Graham wanted to reach out and grab for Christ. If the story of the Laymen's Prayer Revival has touched you and given you new motivation to pray, you might want to use a world map as a guide for prayer. If your world vision has been really stretched take a map and pray for three countries each day, six days a week. At that rate, you can pray around the world in 80 days.

A Final Word of Encouragement

I found the support of a small fellowship group to be a tremendous stimulus to love and serve the Lord. I have also experienced His love through others as we have met on a consistent basis. For these reasons I would like to encourage you to pay whatever price necessary so that you too can meet regularly in the spirit of Christ with a few others like-minded.

The price for most of us falls into four categories:

1. *Too scared.* We develop many mechanisms to protect our egos. The scriptural approach is crucifixion of self. Perhaps your price is to cast off your inhibitions and be willing to experience the crucifixion of egocentric feelings by being open and vulnerable to others.

2. *Too busy.* Most schedules are overloaded and to add something new, something else will have to be replaced. This is a matter of priorities, of being willing to put fellowship high on your priority list.

3. *Too complacent.* Jesus said, "Blessed are those who hunger and thirst for righteousness" (Matt. 5:6). Perhaps the most desperate need among the people in our churches today is the lack of desire to seek Him and to be their best for Him. Right now in prayer you can tell God that you want a spiritual hunger for Him. Then start praying to find a few others likeminded with whom you can join in fellowship.

4. *Too experienced.* Perhaps you have been meeting physically for some time with others and you fall into this category. You have had a great deal of experience but are not excited about your fellowship. Perhaps your price will be to get the companion study guide to this book and work with your group on appropriating these spiritual dynamics. Fellowship in a small group is biblical, fulfilling, encouraging, edifying, and enjoyable.

Wherever you are it is my prayer that you too will find fellowship with others in the Lord Jesus Christ; that together through application of these scriptural principles the flow of His Spirit through you will be increased in service to others.

"Not forsaking our own assembling together, as is the habit of some, but encouraging one another; and all the more, as you see the day drawing near" (Heb. 10:25).

Perhaps if we pray together in love, loving the Lord first and then one another, God might be pleased to cause a spiritual awakening that will burn across our world like a prairie fire out of control. Do it again, Lord! Grant a turning of multitudes to You. . . . Call Your army to active duty so that we might be a part of a great global ingathering of individuals before the return of our Lord Jesus Christ!